Cathedral Grove

M a c M i l l a n   P a r k

Jan Peterson

Cathedral Grove

M a c M i l l a n   P a r k

oolichan books

Lantzville, British Columbia

1996

Oolichan Books would like to thank Steve Zaleschuk of Memories, Port Alberni, B.C. for permission to reproduce his photograph of Cathedral Grove on the cover.

Oolichan Books acknowledges the support received for its publishing program from the Canada Council's Block Grants program, the British Columbia Ministry of Small Business, Tourism and Culture, and the Department of Canadian Heritage.

Canadian Cataloguing in Publication Data
Peterson, Jan, 1937-
  Cathedral Grove (MacMillan Park)

  Includes bibliographical references and index.
  ISBN 0-88982-160-7

  1. Cathedral Grove (B.C.) 2. MacMillan Provincial Park
(B.C.) 3. Old growth forest conservation—British Columbia—
Vancouver Island—History. I. Title.
FC3815.M3P47 1996   333.78'4   C96-910333-6
F1089.M2P47 1996

Published by
Oolichan Books
Box 10
Lantzville, British Columbia
Canada V0R 2H0

Printed in Canada by
MORRISS PRINTING COMPANY LTD.
Victoria, British Columbia

Acknowledgements

In addition to those already listed in the text, I thank my family for their support of my efforts in writing this book. A special thanks to my son John Peterson who guided the photography section of the book and maintained an interest in its overall look. Also my thanks to photographer Rochelle Rooker who contributed her expertise and, with John, spent many hours and days hiking the area around Cathedral Grove in all kinds of weather to achieve the present-day photographs of the park. I'm grateful for the patience and dedication they brought to the task.

I appreciated the help of the Alberni District Historical Society Archives workshop volunteers and the staff of the Alberni Valley Museum who continue to support efforts to record the history of the Alberni Valley. Their dedication to collecting and conservation has made the museum facility one of the best on Vancouver Island and an important first stop for researchers.

Thanks to Dick McMinn (nom-de-plume Pat Grace) and Florence McNeil for their poetry; to friend Dorrit MacLeod for scrutinizing the manuscript; to Sandra Oickle for her darkroom expertise in producing the historical photographs; to Neil Malbon, of MacMillan Bloedel's Alberni Forest Information Centre in Port Alberni, for sharing his knowledge of the park; to George Brandak, Curator of Manuscripts, Special Collections Division, University of British Columbia, for wading through the MacMillan records on my behalf. Also I appreciated the assistance I received from Ron Atterbury, of the *Alberni Valley Times*. A special acknowledgement goes to Shirley Gunderson and Ray Millard of the Chemainus Valley Museum, for going out of their way in efforts in locate photographs for the book. All have contributed greatly.

My thanks to Steve Zaleschuk who contributed the beautiful cover photograph which depicts the very essence of Cathedral Grove, and to designer Jim Bennett and Morriss Printing for the quality of their production. Working with editor Rhonda Bailey and the staff of Oolichan Books has again been a pleasure. I applaud their publishing expertise.

This fallen tree was cut to provide a path through the park.

Preface

I first saw MacMillan Park-Cathedral Grove in 1964. Walking beneath the giants, I was struck by the beauty of the forest. Never before had I seen trees so large, and like many other travellers before me I likened the experience to being in a cathedral, or church. My first impression of the sheer majesty of the giant cedars and Douglas-firs is something I will never forget. Little did I know then I eventually would be living in Port Alberni and would travel through Cathedral Grove many, many times. The easy accessibility of the Grove is a joy.

When I began researching the history of the Albernis for two books on the subject, I noted information about Cathedral Grove and Port Alberni's attempt to have it preserved. My research coincided with the protests on the West Coast of Vancouver Island by preservationists bent on saving the Carmanah forest and changing forest practices in Clayoquot Sound. Port Alberni Mayor Gillian Trumper issued a challenge to the groups: save Cathedral Grove. The tiny park—so easily accessible to everyone—was suffering due to its growing popularity, and the damage to the park's ecosystem was going unnoticed and unchecked.

I realized what a remarkable achievement it had been so many years ago to save Cathedral Grove. The more I learned about the people who made it happen, the more I wanted to write the history of the preservation of this tiny forest seen yearly by thousands of visitors.

The millions of hectares of new parks now being created in British Columbia will never have the same impact on the general public and will be seen by only a limited number of people.

Now there is hope on the horizon for Cathedral Grove. MLA Gerard Janssen (NDP, Alberni) announced in February 1996, the approval of $100,000 to complete the planning for improvements to MacMillan Park, improvements that are expected to reach $1.7 million and will include improved parking and an interpretive centre. This is very good news on the eve of the 50th Anniversary of the dedication of the park.

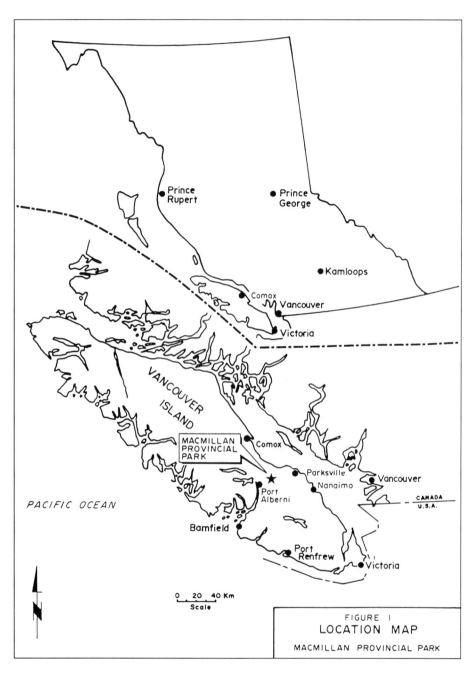

Prince
Rupert

Prince
George

Kamloops

Comox

Vancouver

Victoria

VANCOUVER
ISLAND

MACMILLAN
PROVINCIAL
PARK

Comox

Parksville

Nanaimo

Vancouver

Port
Alberni

CANADA
U.S.A.

PACIFIC OCEAN

Bamfield

Port
Renfrew

Victoria

0   20   40 Km
Scale

FIGURE I
LOCATION MAP

MACMILLAN PROVINCIAL PARK

MAP COURTESY B.C. PARKS

Foreword

Before the Clayoquot Sound protests, before Carmanah, before the Walbran and Meares Island logging conflicts, and before provincial or federal governments took an interest in Canadian forests, one little thirty-acre stand of giant trees in the centre of Vancouver Island became the focus of British Columbia's first fight for the preservation of the forest. Residents and visitors alike all agreed the old-growth forest at Cameron Lake in Central Vancouver Island should be exempt from the logger's axe. The cast of characters involved in the history of the preservation of Cathedral Grove (MacMillan Park) includes some of the province's first movers and shakers in the forest industry. Today over a quarter of a million people from around the world annually walk beneath the giants and experience the coastal forests of British Columbia as they must have been before settlement. This is a testimony to the foresight of countless people who worked and lobbied to bring politicians on side to have the park preserved for future generations.

Cameron Lake Road.   LEONARD FRANK PHOTO

Cathedral Grove, 1924.

Contents

Mt. Arrowsmith. SOURCE MABEL TAYLOR

CAMERON LAKE.
VANCOUVER ISLAND.
B. C.

View of Cameron Lake, 1924.

PART I

Hemlock trees, ferns and fallen younger trees bridge the swollen creek.

Chapter One

WOOD INTERIOR

I live at the top
    of my own cathedral
have painted velvet trees
shaded the walls blue grey
like an Archbishop's robes
on feast days
see heaven through
the sky I stained
with yellow glass
made aisles of ocean ferns
and now alone   grotesque
in my tower
I play the leaves like bells
and hope like Quasimodo
that a face from the crowd
will light up at the beauty
I have made
or God Himself will visit
my cathedral
          FLORENCE MCNEIL,[1] *Emily*

CARVING OUT A FUTURE

*M*ount Arrowsmith sits like a sentinel overlooking the Alberni Valley to the west and the Parksville, Qualicum, and Nanaimo area to the east. This magnificent mountain, 1817 metres high, dominates the landscape in Central Vancouver Island. Indians first named it Kulth-ka-choolth, meaning "jagged face." Later, in 1856, Captain Richards of the Royal Navy, who was commissioned in 1856 by the English government to survey and chart the coast of Vancouver Island, gave the mountain an English name in honour of the English cartographers Aaron and John Arrowsmith.[2]

Ten million years ago, Mount Arrowsmith's peak rose above an ice mass that covered the Island and most of British Columbia. As the climate warmed towards the end of the ice age, glaciers gouged out deep coastal valleys, leaving the province's present topography. The ice slowly moved southwest across the Beaufort Range through the rock-cut basin of the Cameron Valley from the Georgia Depression towards the Alberni Valley.[3] Along Vancouver Island's west coast, the ice created fiord-like inlets that cut deep into the land mass. The Alberni Inlet, forty-eight kilometres long, almost slices the Island in half. Cameron River, which feeds into Cameron Lake, begins twenty-four kilometres southeast, at Labour Day Lake in the Cameron River watershed. The river snakes northwest between McLaughlin Ridge on the west and Mount Moriarty and Mount Arrowsmith on the east, carrying silt and essential nutrients into the Cameron Lake basin by a number of tributary streams including Yellow Creek, Cop Creek, and Kammat Creek.[4]

Skirting the lake's southwestern shore is an area covered by giant trees hundreds of years old. Heavy winter rainfall of 277 mm and mild summer temperatures averaging 17 degrees Celsius support the dense forest growth of the region and provide excellent climatic conditions for the proliferation of Douglas-fir, western hemlock, western redcedar, grand fir, pacific yew, big leaf maple, red alder, dogwood, and black cottonwood. The predominant Douglas-fir trees have an average age of 315 years, but some are estimated to be between five hundred and eight hundred years old. The fir trees were so named for Scottish-born botanist David Douglas, who investigated the flora of western North America. The tallest trees reach about 250 feet. Beneath these giants, whose crowns form a canopy almost impervious to sunlight, is a moss-covered world of sword fern, vanilla leaf, and devil's club. The Cameron River hosts Kokanee salmon as well as rainbow and cutthroat trout.[5]

This rich ecosystem is home to deer, black bear, cougar and the Vancouver Island wolf, and a herd of Roosevelt Elk roams the slopes of Mount Arrowsmith. The forest is also home to bats, squirrels, and short-tailed weasels and is a breeding ground for woodpeckers, chickadees, robins, thrushes, and Steller's jays.

It was also Captain Richards who named Cameron Lake, in recognition of the Honourable David Cameron, chief justice of Vancouver Island. Cameron, the first judge of the colony, was originally a cloth merchant in Perth, Scotland; he came to Vancouver Island in 1853 to work for the Hudson's Bay Company in Nanaimo. He married the sister of James Douglas, chief factor of the Hudson's Bay Company, who later became Governor of Vancouver Island.

The forests of British Columbia are part of a much larger old-growth forest system which curves in an arc from Alaska to San Francisco.[6] The forest remained untouched for thousands of years except to provide shelter, fuel, and food for its first inhabitants, the Native people, who recognized early its value as a home for fur-bearing animals. Even the Hudson's Bay Company, who arrived with a mandate to encourage settlement and development, discouraged clearing the forests because of the company's fur-trading interest.

When the Europeans and Spaniards first explored the west coast of Vancouver Island, they saw an endless wall of forest green from shoreline to mountaintop. Even the islands were dotted with giant cedars, firs, and arbutus trees. One early visitor moaned at the forbidding picture: "I raised my eyes to the sky and could see nothing but the worthless timber that covered everything."[7] The land was forbidding and access was difficult, so most of the Nuu-chah-nulth tribes of the west coast lived on the water's edge. Only the Opetchesaht tribe, residents of the Alberni Valley for thousands of years, were known to travel inland to hunt.[8] They crossed the Central Island using the Horne Lake trail, which started near Qualicum Creek and emerged in the Alberni Valley. There is no evidence showing the Cameron Lake route was ever used. In 1856, Nanaimo Hudson's Bay Company employee Adam Grant Horne pioneered the Horne Lake route for use by settlers when entering the Alberni Valley.[9] Early surveys judged the route unacceptable for a wagon road, and subsequent provincial governments searched for a better route across the island.

The giants of the forest were of great importance to the Nuu-chah-nulth, for although the Native people were isolated between the mountainous rough terrain and the huge swells of the Pacific Ocean, they needed the trees for their homes, their clothing, and especially their canoes. Alfred Carmichael, an early pioneer of the Alberni Valley, described the importance of the trees in the lives of the Tseshaht:

> To the lone Indian, who slowly paddles his canoe upon the waters of this western sound, each tree of different kind by shade of green and shape of crown is known; the Toh-a-mupt or Sitca spruce with scaly bark and prickly spine; the feathery foliage of Quilth-kla-mupt, the western hemlock, relieved in spring by the light green of tender shoots. The frondlike branches and aromatic scent betray to him the much-prized Hohm-ess, the giant cedar tree, from which he carves his staunch canoe. These form the woods which sweep from rocky shore to topmost hill.[10]

The cedar bark was highly prized. In early May, when the new growth appeared, the bark was loosened and pulled from the tree, rolled up, and carried home where it was pounded between stones; then the fibres were softened and woven into clothing. The canoes were carved from a single log of redcedar and used for travelling the coastline from village to village. These impressive cedar vessels were first seen by Europeans when the Indians paddled out to the ships. The best canoes were made by the Clayoquot and Nitinat tribes of the west coast of Vancouver Island.[11]

The mountainous terrain surrounding the Cameron Lake basin made the area quite inaccessible and so remained untouched until a survey in

Young alders screen Cameron River.

Cameron Lake. LEONARD FRANK PHOTO

A cedar and Douglas-fir edge the swollen river.

1861, led by Lieutenant Richard Charles Mayne, RN, happened upon the lake. Mayne left Alberni for Nanoose Bay, following much the same route as the road travels today. He wrote of passing over the Alberni Summit and descending into "a grove of great timber" where he shot an elk. The party came to a "small lake [of] which none of the Indians had any previous knowledge,"[12] then walked along the lake until they were stopped at a rock, or bluff, and decided to camp for the night. The next morning they built a raft and floated down the lake. Their journey from Alberni to Nanaimo via Nanoose Bay on the Island's east coast had taken seven days.

Now there appeared an encroachment upon the endless sea of green. A request by Captain Edward Stamp for a timber allocation in the Alberni Valley resulted in the first forestry debate in the British Columbia legislature. Stamp wanted to secure an area for manufacturing ship spars for export. On March 1, 1860 Governor James Douglas addressed the second House of Assembly for the Colony of Vancouver Island:

> We have also to consider how the colonization of the country, and the development of its resources can best be promoted. With a pleasant, and healthy climate, which on the whole may compare favourably with that of any other country, Vancouver Island also possesses a fertile soil; forests of vast extent; a sea coast abounding in fish, and studded with safe and convenient Harbours; extensive coal beds; and the unoccupied lands of the Crown form a wide and varied domain, and we have to consider how those sources of wealth are to be developed and to be made of value to the Colony.

> I will, hereafter, lay before you the copy of a correspondence with Captain Stamp, a gentleman representing a highly respectful English association which proposes to form a settlement at some eligible point on the West Coast of Vancouver Island for the purpose of establishing fisheries, and of entering largely into the manufacture and export of deals and ships' spars. If the results obtainable through those industrial pursuits may be estimated from the number of ships employed, and the amount of capital invested in the fisheries and timber trade in the British Provinces of North America, we shall at once perceive their extraordinary value and importance.[13]

One month later, on April 2, 1860 in the same House of Assembly the following resolution was entered:

> That this House do resolve itself into a Committee of the whole to consider and report on the application of Captain Stamp to His Excellency the Governor for permission to cut timber, establish saw Mills and to purchase farming lands in the vicinity of Barclay Sound on the West Coast of this Island.[14]

Stamp was so impressed by the great Island forests that he convinced two English shipping companies to back him in the sawmill venture. The companies had been accustomed to purchasing spars and timber in the United States, but with the Civil War imminent they were anxious to secure an alternative supply source. The legislature granted 2000 acres to build a settlement and another 15,000 acres of forest for the sawmill.

Stamp established the Anderson Sawmill in what became known as Alberni in 1860. The site was abandoned when the mill ran out of easily accessible timber within four years as the mechanization did not exist to transport the huge logs to the mills.[15]

The Canadian Pacific Railway's trans-continental passenger service reached Vancouver in 1886. From the Atlantic and points beyond, the passenger trains brought settlers intent on carving out a living from the land. Forests were considered an impediment to be cleared away or burned to allow for agriculture development. Already the forests in Eastern Canada had seen the logger's axe. There the early forest industry depended on men, oxen, and water to get the trees from the woods to the rivers. Every spring, when water levels rose, hazardous river drives were held to float the logs to the mills in Ontario, Quebec, and the Atlantic provinces. Shipbuilding helped stimulate the industry, which in turn brought capital investment, fees, and regulations—detriments to many of the small independent logging operators.[16] Professional forestry and conservation lay in the future.

Across Canada and all along the Canadian railway belt, fires burned as trees were felled to make way for settlement. Alberni Valley settler Kenneth McKenzie remembers the high-grade Douglas-fir trees being felled and bucked into two-foot lengths which were then split to be used in burning out the stumps. As it was necessary to keep the fires burning twenty-four hours a day, the family took turns stoking the fires during the night. "The air was constantly thick with smoke in the valley, as the settlers cleared their property."[17]

The CPR began an intensive advertising campaign to entice tourists into these new and scenic areas. Soon Banff National Park in Alberta and Glacier and Yoho National Parks in British Columbia were established within the railway land.[18]

When the number of settlers increased in the Alberni Valley, the government allocated money for a wagon road to Nanaimo. The sixty-mile, ten-foot-wide roadway wound around the eastern shore of Cameron Lake, thus avoiding the huge rock mass encountered by Mayne years earlier. Road building proved difficult due to rock slides and boulders falling from the steep hillside. When completed in November 1886, the road remained in poor condition with stumps and roots clearly visible. Wheeled vehicles were unable to use it during part of the winter. Bridges were built over Qualicum River, French Creek and Englishman River.

Events taking place elsewhere had great implications for the future of the giant trees of Cathedral Grove. On August 13, 1886, at Shawnigan Lake in the south Vancouver Island region, Sir John A. Macdonald drove the last spike on the Esquimalt & Nanaimo Railway. The railway, built by a consortium headed by the Honourable Robert Dunsmuir, a leading coal industrialist from Nanaimo, linked Victoria to Nanaimo. The Dominion Government granted Dunsmuir concessions to build the railway; these included a grant of 1,900,000 acres of land. Twenty miles wide, this strip of land stretching from Esquimalt almost to Campbell River became known as the E&N Land Grant. The Cameron Lake basin lay within the land grant, and now the destiny of the giant trees was in the hands of private industry.

Chapter Two

The wonder of the world,
The Beauty and the Power,
The Shapes of things, their colours
Lights and shades, these I saw.
Look ye also while life lasts.

ANON.[19]

DR. JAMES FLETCHER

*T*he first known public expression of a desire to preserve this natural treasure came from James Fletcher, the first Dominion entomologist and botanist.[20] In 1871 at the age of nineteen, Fletcher, of Kent, England, began working in the London branch of the Bank of Britain, and later transferred to Ottawa, Canada. He left the bank in 1876 to accept a position with the Parliamentary Library. In his leisure hours, he studied botany and entomology, and frequently gave advice to the Department of Agriculture. The government soon recognized his expertise, and on June 1, 1883, he was appointed honourary entomologist to the Department of Agriculture. He prepared his first report in December 1884 and a new one each succeeding year until his death in 1908.[21] Accolades followed Fletcher as his reputation spread across Canada. His marriage in 1879 to Eleanor Gertrude, daughter of Sir Collingwood Schreiber, produced two daughters, Constance and Dorothy.

On a speaking tour of Farmers' Institutes in British Columbia, in August 1901, Fletcher explored the Cameron Lake-Mount Arrowsmith area; he climbed Mount Arrowsmith with the help of Alberni Tseshaht Indian guide John Clutesi and Scotsman Rob McKinley. Accompanying him were friends James Robert Anderson, British Columbia's Deputy Minister of Agriculture and superintendent of British Columbia Farmers' Institutes, and the Reverend George Taylor of Wellington, B.C. Anderson, who was one of the first members of the Natural History Society of British Columbia, had, in 1890, collected and donated rare British Columbia plants to the Department of Agriculture. The Reverend Taylor, an amateur naturalist, entomologist, and marine scientist, also donated a collection of Vancouver Island insects.

There seemed little of importance to record about the trio's visit to Alberni as evidenced by Anderson's diary entry of Monday, August 5, 1901. "Left French Creek abt 8—Lunched at Cameron Lake and reached Alberni abt 5. Had meeting in evg."[22] Anderson claimed later it was he who first suggested the Cameron Lake forest be saved from the logger's axe. He certainly was a student of natural history and had a great love for British Columbia, a love he learned from his father Alexander C. Anderson, Collector of Customs and Postmaster pro tem, who was also something of a botanist. All his life James collected and pressed plants; plants, trees, and shrubs were his hobby. Unfortunately, his work went unrecognized. One of his best collections, after being offered to British Columbia and refused, was later sold to Washington State University. He made one of the earliest reports on the tree life of British Columbia ever submitted to the Dominion Government.[23]

The trio met with the Farmers' Institute regarding government help in clearing away the stumps of gigantic trees which were getting in the way of farming in the Alberni Valley. Unlike other provinces, in British Columbia the Farmers' Institute was a relatively new development. Fletcher noted Alberni already had an active organization. Farmers viewed Fletcher's visit with great interest, and he noted that the farmers came to the meeting "knowing what they want, and are prepared to put their views plainly before the meeting."[24] Anderson announced his government had made arrangements to provide gunpowder at half the price if the farmers conformed to rules and regulations. Fletcher gave his "Nature Study" speech, which related to a new educational movement he claimed would be of value to local farmers. In his speech Fletcher also urged preservation of the forest at Cameron Lake.

> Speaking of the great interest now being created in forestry by the new Canadian Forestry Association, I urge you to do everything in your power to preserve the magnificent forest around Cameron Lake, within a few miles of Alberni. I believe this is one of the finest pieces of standing timber in the world. The very size of the trees as up to the present there are no railways there, would protect it for many years if you could keep out the greatest enemy of all—fire. There are few places where trees of from five to eight feet in diameter could be seen, as is the case there, by thousands. Everyone should do something to create an interest in this subject, if not, indeed, on occasion, to prevent fire from spreading.[25]

Fletcher reminded his audience that a single spark would be enough to start a "disastrous conflagration." Both he and Anderson were concerned about the vast timber tracts being consumed by fire.[26] On Fletcher's return trip, the party climbed Mount Arrowsmith, a camping expedition that took four days, allowing lots of time to examine the plant life of the mountain.

James Robert Anderson.

James Fletcher. Detail from National Archives of Canada, #C9232.

The Reverend George Taylor.

Low light and intermittent flooding keep undergrowth to a minimum.

Fletcher wrote to his sister Flory about the trip:

We walked four and half miles to the base of the mountain. Here we crossed the Cameron River by the means of a convenient tree, a giant of 150 feet which had fallen right across. In this way we saved ourselves wading up to our knees in a raging glacial torrent, as cold as liquid ice and coming straight down from a glacier up on the top of old Arrowsmith. We then began a terrific climb of six solid hours without a drop of water. Our tongues were about like bricks and we had not much appetite for supper. We pitched camp at 7:00 p.m. and had a most delightful cool night, almost frost but with a roaring fire in front of our camp, and slept on about two feet of deliciously scented spruce boughs.[27]

The next morning the trio climbed another two miles over the ridge of the mountain up to the main peak, which Fletcher described as "a stupendous mass of rock, about as big as 10 St. Paul's cathedrals." They found some new plants before returning to camp for another evening. The following day Fletcher collected bunches of red and white heather, then began the descent by a new trail. Horses were waiting for the group when they reached the bottom of the mountain the next morning.

Fletcher's visit with the Alberni Valley farmers and his noted concern for the preservation of the forest at Cameron Lake did not create any memorable impression on the Island farmers who were more concerned with clearing away the stumps of giant trees to make way for agricultural land than preserving the forest at Cameron Lake, or elsewhere. There was no ground-swell of public opinion favouring Fletcher's plea for preservation, but the thought, or seed, had been firmly planted in Alberni.

Licorice fern growing on a moss-covered tree.

Chapter Three

DEEP WOODS

Among tall trees
the game-trails run,
padded with needles
making the soft silence
of deep woods. The sun
is almost lost but shows
in long slants
draped through limbs
like ghost-fingers
through giant plants.
There is a silence here
that is almost heard,
moving in a mossy world
where time is stopped
and living blurred.
There is no medicine
like these—
The quiet touch of
Tall, tall trees!

PAT GRACE

OPENING UP THE FORESTS FOR INVESTMENT

*T*he Canadian Forestry Association, formed in 1900 to "promote forestry in Canada,"[28] first expressed concern about the rapid decline of timber supply and passed a resolution "That all lands found unfit for agriculture purposes be declared forest lands and kept as such in perpetuity."[29] The group also expressed concern about railways passing through coniferous forests and the "serious danger of loss of valuable timber."[30]

In 1903, when Richard McBride became Premier of British Columbia, the provincial government made little money from forestry, quite unlike the forest activity taking place to the south in Washington and Oregon. Provincial revenue for the year from leased and licensed timberland stood at only $300,000.[31] To boost provincial coffers, McBride threw open all forest lands to speculators who could purchase as many timber licences as they wanted. The only government requirement was that they pay an annual interest fee on the value of the timber cut. After a period of two years, the lands could be resold.

Martin Allerdale Grainger, the author of the first B.C. Forest Act, described this period of speculation in his 1908 book *Woodsmen of the West*:

> In British Columbia, you should know, a man could go anywhere on unoccupied Crown lands, put in a corner post, compose a rough description of one square mile of forest measured from that post, and thus secure from the Government exclusive right to the timber on that square mile, subject to the payment of a rent of one hundred and forty dollars a year ("No Chinese or Japanese to be employed in working the timber"). Such a square mile of forest is known as a "timber claim."[32]

These Special Timber Licences (S.T.L.s) looked inviting to investors, many of whom were from the United States, where forest lands had already been plundered. John D. Rockefeller Jr. of New York purchased 18,000 acres of the rich Ash River Valley, north of Alberni. The Red Cliff Land and Lumber Company of Duluth, Minnesota, purchased 30,000 acres in the Alberni Valley. In 1907, the Alberni government office reported a record 1200 timber licences filed from April to August.[33] Provincial revenue from forests had increased to $1.3 million by 1907, but because the province was losing its forests at an alarming rate it ended the lucrative licensing and leasing systems.

Upon the death of Robert Dunsmuir in 1889, his son James became the sole owner of the Esquimalt & Nanaimo Railway (E&N). This same year, the Victoria Lumber & Manufacturing Company (VL&MC), in Chemainus, acquired 7 per cent of the E & N land grant which included Block 35 from the E&N Railway.[34] Block 35, containing some of the largest trees in Cathedral Grove, lay within the Nanaimo Regional District and only a few kilometres from the Albernis. In 1905, Dunsmuir sold the railway with all assets, including the remaining E&N Land Grant, to the Canadian Pacific Railway Company (CPR). The new owner retained the original name of E&N Railway and looked to further its investment and open up the land by extending the rail lines to the north and west Island. The extension of the line to Parksville was completed first. From there, the line divided, went west to Port Alberni and eventually north to Courtenay.

In 1907, the Alberni Land Company, owners of the Alberni townsite, concluded a deal with the CPR to extend their line to Alberni in return for 2,500 acres of the townsite land for railway development. This was an important business agreement for the area, particularly for the Barclay

Sound Cedar Company sawmill producing lumber for export. A rail link to the east coast of the Island would boost sales to Eastern markets.

The railway first reached the eastern end of Cameron Lake in 1909, and at mile 12.7, almost half-way between Parksville and Alberni, the CPR built the beautiful Cameron Lake Chalet, which became a resort destination for visitors from around the world for the next five decades. Until the remainder of the railway was built, travellers destined for the Albernis were picked up by a horse-drawn stagecoach.

Today little remains of the beautiful chalet that once offered accommodation and recreational facilities in conjunction with day-to-day railway functions. The resort opened from May 1 to October 15. The chalet, with spacious verandahs on all sides overlooking the lake and surrounding mountains, was the place to see and be seen. Travellers journeying from the east coast to the Albernis dropped in for tea and rubbed elbows with lords and ladies with their accompanying servants. Lunches and Sunday dinners were popular events attracting a clientele from the Central Island region.

The main building had five bedrooms on two floors for guests. The Victorian design furniture was dark, heavy and square, and quite ornate. Beds were large with high headboards; each room came equipped with a washstand and the traditional set of chinaware pitcher and washbasin. Pieces of this furniture are presently displayed in the Alberni Valley Museum in Port Alberni.

A baggage room faced the railway track. In the dining room, located on the south end of the building, tables were adorned with embroidered tablecovers and set with china in the blue willow pattern—a Chinese design featuring a scene of bridges, birds and trees—so popular during this period. During the busy summer season, when the chalet filled with visitors, a line of tents between the house and lake accommodated the overflow.

The CPR recognized the tourism value of Cameron Lake, the giant trees in the Cameron River valley, and Mount Arrowsmith, and it seemed for a time the area would become a major resort destination point on Vancouver Island. The original chalet managers were Mr. and Mrs. A. M. Monks. Mr. Monks also served as a hunting and fishing guide. He loved the mountain and envisioned great things for the CPR if Mount Arrowsmith were developed for recreation; the view from the summit was stunning and could be reached with a minimum of effort and expense.

The CPR surveyed and developed a good trail clearly marked by small cairns built of stones. Should a hiker encounter fog, he could easily follow the way down. A cabin, built on the timberline about eight miles from the chalet, was furnished with a good cookstove, cooking utensils, dishes, and items necessary for a comfortable short stay. Several pack-

Road construction, north side of Cameron Lake, 1895.

Last stagecoach through Cathedral Grove, 1911.
PHOTO COURTESY DAVID WILSON

Cameron Lake forest, 1913.

Right-of-way
construction
of the E&N Railway,
1909-1910.

AVM PN 877

AVM PN 917

AVM PN 1032

Peak of Mt. Arrowsmith.
LEONARD FRANK PHOTO

Location Survey, E&N Railway, 1903.

E&N Railway near Alberni Summit, 1913.   LEONARD FRANK PHOTO

First Port Alberni passenger train stops at Cameron Lake in 1911.

Road winding around Cameron Lake, 1920.
JOSEPH CLEGG PHOTO

Tourist cabin tents at
Cameron Lake Chalet.

Frank J. D. Barnjum.
Photo from *B.C. News*,
November 1959, published
by B.C. House,
London, England.

Survey crew, E&N Railway, 1908. Identified are
Joe Garvin, Bob Lees and Brent Morriss.

horses were on hand so that tourists had nothing to carry, and if they wished they could travel on horseback as far as the cabin.[35]

George Bird, a pioneer sawmill operator in Port Alberni, wrote of the view from the cabin:

> The whole of the Straits of Georgia, from Cape Mudge down to the Gulf Islands lies in view below. The Comox District, English Bay and Vancouver are seen. From the cabin at night we could see the bright lights of the settlement on Texada Island, where the large kilns burning lime are at work. It is necessary to choose a time before the bush and logging camp fires start, and when it is warm, fine weather, or clouds may be encountered. The Pacific Ocean is in view on a clear day. The Albernis are very plainly seen; even the streets and large buildings can be picked out.

> Down in the valley between the first peak and the main mountain, I suppose nearly 5,000 feet above sea level, lies a picturesque little lake, with the greenest of green water, as seen from above on a fine day. In July and August there are snowbanks in places and it is quite a novelty to have a bit of a snowball fight at that time of year. On the far side of the first peak, as you reach the top, there is an awe-inspiring precipice. There must be a sheer drop of at least two to three thousand feet of a perpendicular cliff.[36]

According to Bird, celebrated mountaineer Edward Whymper, the first person to climb the Matterhorn, climbed Mount Arrowsmith sometime between 1901 and 1905. The Whymper cairn, once located on the summit, has since disappeared, but the legendary climb is not forgotten.

The start of the mountain recreation venture appeared destined for success. Then the First World War interceded. Two years into the war, Mr. Monks joined the service and went overseas. He was killed in action in 1917. The high hopes held by the Monks for the resort died with him. Mrs. Monks never recovered from her husband's death, and in 1920 Mr. and Mrs. George Woollett of Port Alberni took over the management of the Chalet. They continued to operate it successfully for many years.

Building a railway across the Beaufort Mountain range into the Alberni Valley was not an easy task. The CPR first had to build a new road along the southern side of Cameron Lake, allowing the rail tracks to be laid along the old wagon road hugging the sheer cliffs several feet above the water on the northern side of the lake. The new road lengthened the distance to Nanaimo by a mile and a half. The Calgary firm of Jannse, McDonnell, and Timothy received the contract to grade the last twenty-seven miles to Alberni. Hundreds of men were employed constructing and grading with picks and shovels. The new road was carved out of the massive rockface nicknamed Angel Rock, and some giant Douglas-firs of Cameron forest were felled to accommodate the transportation link. For the first time, travellers could easily see the magnificent "old-growth"[37] trees. The sight of these giants of the forest left many travellers speechless. So breathtaking was the sight, one visitor, Mrs. Buxton, compared the forest to St. Paul's Cathedral in London, England.[38] This may have been the first recorded time the experience of being in the old-growth forest was likened to being in a cathedral.

Businessman Edward T. Buxton, director of the Red Cliff Land and Lumber Company Ltd., recorded in his journal his impressions of travelling through the forest with his wife, en route to Alberni where his company intended to purchase large tracts of timber from the CPR. They started their journey in Nanaimo in the early morning in order to cross the mountain pass by daylight. Partelow Miles, the company representative in Alberni, picked up the couple in an English Humber automobile. Buxton wrote:

> The road for about seventy miles is almost straight and through a virgin forest of Douglas fir. The rise in the elevation is gradual but continuous. The trees are from two to three hundred feet in height, straight as a lance and most symmetrical in shape, with no branches for the first one hundred or one hundred and fifty feet. The tops are like a huge plume of very dark green foliage. The soughing of the wind through the trees and the gentle swaying of the tops and branches is most impressive. So graceful, so perfectly symmetrical are they that it is difficult to realize their great size. There is no underbrush but a dense carpet of ferns covers the ground beneath. The road stretches for miles before one; shaded like an avenue by the dense forest. There is an occasional view of a snowclad mountain top in the distance.

> No sound save the purr of the motor or an occasional scream of a mountain lion or the whir of a grouse or a Chinese pheasant. The deer stand by the roadside, too curious to move and quite indifferent, yet as we speed swiftly by, they jump into the forest, startled by the rapid movement of the car. Several times we noticed ahead of us in the roadway, bears which would leisurely shamble into the woods. After about seventy miles, the road begins to wind and there are frequent and continual steep pitches, until we reach a beautiful mountain lake, in a narrow valley in the mountains. Steep cliffs on three sides and high mountains all about. The lake is fed by water from the snow clad peaks and the glacier on Mount Arrowsmith.

> The road winds about the shore of the lake and in and about a grove of magnificent fir trees. The trees are from three hundred and fifty feet in height and have all the symmetry and beauty of the smaller firs and the grandeur of their gigantic size. As our motor runs silently over the thick carpet of pine needles with which the road is covered, we are in the twilight of evening, although it is scarcely past mid-day. We are all silent, awed by this most impressive spectacle. The motor stops. I looked at Mrs. Buxton, tears were on her cheeks. At length she spoke. "Do you remember being in St. Paul's Cathedral in London during a most impressive service with wonderful music. We were in the choir loft. We thought of the generations of our forefathers who had worshipped God in this wonderful edifice and our hearts were full with the majesty and awe of the surroundings. You tell me these trees are from six to seven hundred years old, and I feel their beauty and majesty as I did that of old St. Paul's—God made them."

> We now climb rapidly until the pass is reached at an elevation of about sixteen hundred feet, then a rapid descent of about six miles to sea level at the head of

the fjord at Alberni. We have never forgotten this experience. We know now why genuine woodsmen are a quiet folk.[39]

Alberni residents were buzzing with excitement and speculation in 1907 when W. E. Knapp, general manager of the Red Cliff Land and Lumber Company, arrived in town at the same time as Richard Marpole of the CPR. Their excitement became real after events unfolded showing Knapp had purchased land from the CPR to build a sawmill.[40] Four years later, all the speculation had subsided as the company had still to invest in a plant. President A. E. Gilbert advised the time was not right.[41] The time never was right for the Red Cliff Land and Lumber Company. It eventually sold its timber holdings in the early twenties to Howard A. Dent, a San Francisco lumberman, who had since leased the Alberni Pacific Lumber Company, the former Barclay Sound Cedar Company.[42]

In 1910, an eighteen-year-old British gentleman, later knighted as Sir Henry Gerard Thornton for his work in soil microbiology, set off on a journey across Canada to Vancouver Island. Thornton travelled with his father, F. H. Thornton, and kept faithful records of their journey. They arrived in Vancouver on August 25, then spent several days exploring Thetis Island and visiting young Henry's Uncle Harry. Early in September they hired a "large Daimler motor car" to take them to Alberni.

Young Thornton described the road as "the worst I have seen of similar length," adding that "it is considered, however, by local members of the party to be a 'superb' road."[43] Describing their journey through Cathedral Grove, he noted "the trees become very tall, and there is sometimes just room for the car to pass between two tree-stumps." On the journey to Alberni on the "superb" road, a front spring broke on the car. Not everyone raved happily about their journey through the Grove.

If the Grove needed an advocate at this time, it had found one in J. R. Anderson, secretary of the Natural History Society in Victoria. Anderson spoke out at every opportunity in support of preserving the forest at Cathedral Grove. He prepared a resolution in co-operation with the Vancouver Island Development League. The League sent the resolution to all its branches for endorsement. It stated:

The supplies of wood appear inexhaustible in their natural state, but this is not the case. We have a grand heritage in our noble forests. It would be wise now, before it is too late, to prevent destruction of the pristine beauty. We intend to use every effort to induce the authorities to make such provisions. It is also to insure ourselves those who follow have at least a remnant of our grand forests. Within easy reach by wagon road and soon by rail are the magnificent primeval forests that surround Cameron Lake. It is a representative specimen of our forests wealth which includes streams and mountains within five to 10 square miles. From atop Mount Arrowsmith there is a panoramic view of the north and south ranges, including the Alberni Valley, Barclay Sound, the straits of Georgia and the mainland.

The newly re-organized Nanaimo Board of Trade on November 10, 1911 supported the league in its resolution.[44]

The railway from the Parksville junction to Port Alberni stretched over thirty-eight miles, climbing from sea level through the Cameron Valley to an elevation of 1,284 feet at Locharkaig Summit seventeen miles inland, before beginning the descent. Several high trestles were built along the mountainous terrain. A section house with living room, kitchen, and several bedrooms to accommodate those working on the railway was located at the water stop near the summit. The Bainbridge station, about eight miles from Port Alberni, lasted into the fifties.[45]

The last stagecoach to pick up passengers at the Cameron Lake Chalet rode through Cathedral Grove in 1911 when the E&N Railway reached the Alberni Inlet.

Angel Wings on their host tree.

Chapter Four

"We must strive to touch the land gently
and care for it as true stewards, that
those who follow us and assess our record may
see that our mark on the land was one of
respect and love, not cruelty and disdain."

ROBERT B. OETTING[46]

H. R. MacMILLAN

*I*n 1909, the Canadian Forestry Association (CFA) received a letter from R. H. H. Alexander of Vancouver asking for changes to the Association's constitution to allow for a provincial branch and "thus create in British Columbia a greater interest in the subject of preserving the forest wealth."[47] Another sixteen years passed before the British Columbia Forestry Association formed. At the CFA annual convention held in Victoria on September 4, 1912, Sir Richard McBride opened the proceedings that included delegates from across Canada as well as the Honourable W. R. Ross, Minister of Lands and Forests for British Columbia. One resolution endorsed by the convention established a course in logging engineering at the new University of British Columbia. The new Chief Forester of British Columbia, H. R. MacMillan, guest speaker at the Friday evening social, spoke on "the value of B.C.'s forests."[48]

As a young Ontario forestry student attending Yale University, Harvey Reginald MacMillan saw British Columbia forests for the first time in 1907 when he was hired at $75 a month, plus expenses, as a timber cruiser for the Lindsay syndicate of Ontario to "survey and secure twenty square miles of timber."[49] He returned to university in the fall of the same year having staked thirteen claims and witnessed the best of British Columbia forests. A year later he became ill with tuberculosis. About this time in his life, MacMillan wrote:

> I took a post-graduate course in tuberculosis. It was a shocking thing. On the eve of getting to work, after getting through university, to find that I was sick. It was even worse to be told very soon that I might not get better. And that if I did get better it would be a matter of two or three years.[50]

Following his recovery and subsequent marriage to his childhood sweetheart, Edna Mulloy, MacMillan accepted an offer in 1912 to become

British Columbia's first chief forester at a salary of $2,400 a year. Mac-Millan's mother, Joanna, and his wife, Edna, and their newborn baby, Marion, joined him in Victoria. Another daughter, Jean, was born there in 1915.

Just prior to MacMillan's arrival in British Columbia a Royal Commission on Forestry resulted in the B.C. Forest Act of 1912 being drawn up. Martin Allerdale Grainger had spent two years preparing the legislation that established modern-day forestry practices. Grainger, originally from England, had tried his hand at various occupations, including logging and writing. He settled in Esquimalt with his new bride Mabel and taught for about a year at St. Margaret's School for Girls in Victoria before securing a job as secretary of the royal commission studying forestry. With his knowledge of mathematics and statistics, combined with his writing talent and forest experience, he produced the report and drafted the new Forest Act. The report gave a promising view of inexhaustible timber supplies which would forever sustain the provincial economy.[51]

The Minister of Lands and Forests, the Honourable W. R. Ross, supported his work. Ross condemned the "cut and get out" mentality of foresters. He said, "An epoch, sir, is drawing to a close—the epoch of reckless devastation of the natural resources with which we, the people of this fair young Province, have been endowed by the Providence."[52] Under the new legislation, the British Columbia Forest Service was established. The act provided for fire prevention, fire fighting, sales, log scaling, and royalties, and for the concept of forests being a renewable resource, an idea well ahead of its time. MacMillan, only twenty-two years of age and still looking somewhat fragile, spoke with authority when he gave his speech to the CFA convention. The measures he later implemented made British Columbia a leader in forest management and earned him the respect of everyone.

At the convention were several delegates who would influence the life of the young forester. Papers on forestry issues were presented during the three-day convention, including one from Edmund James Palmer on the subject "Economy in Manufacture." Nicknamed "Old Hickory," Palmer managed the Victoria Lumber & Manufacturing Company (VL&MC) in Chemainus, the owners of Block 35, which included Cathedral Grove. He was also president of the B.C. Lumber & Shingle Manufacturers Association. He joined the company the year following its incorporation in 1889 under owner John Alexander Humbird, a Wisconsin lumberman.[53] Palmer arrived in Chemainus directly from a job as a train conductor.

Humbird had intended to build a mill in Victoria, so he added the name "Victoria" to the new mill. The distinctive trademark of the company, the letter "V" in a diamond, became known throughout the world. MacMillan's and Palmer's paths would cross again.

A survey of British Columbia forest lands progressed and by 1914, 415 forest rangers were employed.[54] One year later the British Columbia forest reserves under provincial jurisdiction were estimated at 2.4 million acres.[55] For the first time, forestry started to be recognized as a profession. British Columbia established the first provincial park in 1911 at Strathcona on Vancouver Island and followed it with Mount Robson Park in 1913.

During the First World War MacMillan became special trade commissioner to Great Britain and found a familiar ally in the new British Columbia trade agent in London, Sir Richard McBride. Together they convinced the United Kingdom Board of Trade to purchase lumber from Canada rather than the United States. MacMillan serviced the contracts through the Forestry Service and gained valuable experience in the export trade. For eighteen months he toured Europe, South Africa, China, and Japan to sell the idea that Douglas-fir was cheaper and better. Many of the importers he met on his tour had been purchasing their lumber through United States firms and were unaware the product had come from Canada.

The CFA began to look ahead to a time after the war when Europe would be looking to North America for wood supplies. The war constituted an irresistible argument in favour of forest conservation in this country. The CFA noted, "If we are to take advantage of the opportunity after the war, it could not be done by the present policy of throwing into the bonfire several times the amount of timber cut annually for our use."[56]

In 1916 MacMillan received an offer from E. J. Palmer to be his assistant manager at VL&MC sawmill in Chemainus. MacMillan now wanted out of public service, and the job offer paid slightly more than he had received from the province. The CFA minute book noted MacMillan's resignation as Chief Forester: "The services of Mr. MacMillan to his province were of the highest order and it is a matter of gratification to know that the new government has appointed the Acting Chief Forester, Mr. M. A. Grainger, to take his place."[57] Grainger held the position of Chief Forester for four years before entering the business world as managing director of the Timber Industries Council, a forestry lobby group.[58] Later he formed the Forest Investment Company with MacMillan as one of his shareholders.

MacMillan began learning the sawmill business. The VL&MC mill was one of the largest in British Columbia and the first logging company to use steam railway in the forest. The company sold lumber to markets around the world and owned some of the finest forests on Vancouver Island. "I have seldom seen such a beautiful Douglas-fir forest as the Victoria Lumber & Manufacturing Company possessed. However, this is

E&N Railway Station at Cameron Lake, *c.* 1920.

View of Cameron Lake from railway.
LEONARD FRANK PHOTO

A railway inspection car and officials
of the E&N Railway.

A Douglas-fir and cedar grow side-by-side.

what one would expect, knowing that it was the first selection any timber cruisers had the opportunity to make out of about one and one half million acres of Douglas-fir forest between Shawnigan Lake and Campbell River."[59]

What enthusiasm MacMillan first had for his new position began to dampen somewhat when his working conditions were realized. "I had no car, no spare time and no holidays. I was expected to put in a full seven-day week. I took inventory on Sundays in the inventory season, finishing it on New Year's Day. No overtime was ever paid to anyone."[60]

Palmer, then over sixty years old, took little interest in the company and was a tough task-master. He rarely went into the woods and seldom went into the mill. MacMillan reminisced about one incident involving the Chinese who worked at the mill:

> I remember once it snowed all night and in the morning there was more than a foot of damp snow. The "old man," "EJ," came to the office in high boots and a bad temper. He growled at me and said "Mac," go up to Chinatown and cut the Chinamen's pay 2c an hour." This meant they would get only 8c an hour instead of 10c." We had 200 to 300 Chinese living in two big "China Houses" where they had individual bunks and got their meals in community kettles.[61]

MacMillan noted the Chinese boss showed no emotion when he received the message.

Within a year Palmer's and MacMillan's personalities clashed and MacMillan resigned; some say he was fired. In a later interview he recalled his feelings at that time: "My boss was twice as old and I had a young man's ideas and they didn't go down too well. So I went out into the world in a hell of a despondent state of mind."[62] As he left the manager's office, MacMillan vowed to return. "When I come through this door again, I'll own this ----- outfit." In 1946 he purchased the company and the old, battered door was duly rehung so MacMillan could walk through it, thus fulfilling his prophecy.

He began working for the Imperial Munitions Board finding Sitka spruce for building aircraft. Out of a job when the war ended, MacMillan decided to enter into a business partnership with Montague Meyer, a timber salesman from London. Both partners put up $10,000 each to start the company. MacMillan borrowed on his house for his share. Under the agreement, Meyer would sell all the timber contracted from MacMillan in B.C. The H. R. MacMillan Export Company Ltd. became incorporated as a private B.C. company in July 1919.

Edmund J. Palmer, manager
of Victoria Lumber &
Manufacturing Co. Ltd.

Martin Allerdale Grainger.

Port Alberni News, August 13, 1919.

A young tree emerges from a springboard-marked stump.

Chapter Five

When all the light
Of daybreak spills,
I see the trees
Walk down the hills

And when dusk fades
The skies of men,
I see the trees
Walk up again.

And sometimes
In the midst of talk,
I wonder
If that silent walk

Has words, or songs,
That fill the air,
And there are those
who care!

PAT GRACE

CALLS FOR PRESERVATION

*T*he notion of preserving the giant trees of Cameron Lake lay dormant until 1919 when a letter to Port Alberni City Council from the Natural History Society of British Columbia, in Victoria, renewed the subject. James Robert Anderson, now vice-president of the Society and the former Deputy Minister of Agriculture, noted how years before he had realized the value of forests and had brought to the attention of authorities the desirability of preserving the Grove as a national heritage. Anderson wanted the forest preserved and dedicated as a lasting memorial to those who had lost their lives in the First World War. "All other suggestions such as monuments erected by the hand of man fade into insignificance when compared to this natural monument erected by the hand of God."[63]

Anderson quoted from a speech he had given while attending a meeting of the CFA in Ottawa, urging the society to help in the preservation of the Cameron Lake forest.

In conclusion, let me say to those members of the Canadian Forestry Association who have not visited the west, that they have yet to see a forest in all its magnificence, and no other word seems to me to convey a proper idea of a virgin forest of the west. Picture to yourself thousands of trees, Douglas-fir predominating, of prodigious size, so close together that it is with difficulty and often impossible for an animal to go between; limbless, except the tops, through which the rays of the sun scarcely penetrate, the ground carpeted with mosses and ferns, and the hush of nature all around you, and you can, perhaps form some idea of this forest in British Columbia.

The CFA adopted Anderson's motion urging the authorities to take action, but no action was forthcoming.

The Natural History Society wanted to save the forest at Cameron Lake but had been unable to get the government interested. It claimed the area had been "alienated" to a logging company who proposed to cut everything down on both sides of the highway.

Port Alberni Alderman B. I. Hart responded to the letter believing something had to be done soon to guarantee the Grove's preservation, or it would be too late. He had been told the owners of the forest were preparing to "turn axe men loose among it. This will be a calamity to this district. There is not to be found anywhere in the world a more beautiful natural park." Hart urged council, the Boards of Trade, and other public organizations, to write to the government to obtain public control.[64] Council voted "to give every support to the movement (to save the forest) and to request the support of Mr. Clements, MP, Mr. Burde MLA, and the Port Alberni Board of Trade."[65]

A year later, in November 1920, George D. Fuller, assistant professor of botany at the University of Chicago, wrote to the Victoria Board of Trade also pleading for preservation of "admittedly the most magnificent Douglas fir forest in the world."[66] Fuller suggested a park be created to include Cameron Lake, Mount Arrowsmith and several square miles of forest.

Often nature can cause more harm than man, as a storm a few months later showed. A hurricane windstorm hit British Columbia on January 29, 1921 and did more damage on Vancouver Island than in any other part of the province. Timber cruisers estimated damage of between 5 and 10 per cent of the best timber on the Island had been destroyed by the hurricane.[67]

The storm cut a swath several hundred yards wide through the Cameron River valley levelling everything in its path. Thousands of the mighty giants were uprooted and the Island highway was scattered with the finest timber. At the time of the storm, timber cruisers were working to decide the amount of forest that would be required to provide a perpetual monument. E. J. Palmer had made a proposition to the government to have the forest protected. The timber cruisers spent the night in government cabins at Cameron River, just over the Beaufort Summit, and narrowly escaped death. Five men were in the cabin and four were in the stable when the storm brought trees crashing down upon the stable. After their rescue, the men left a brief record of their experience written on a large tree alongside the road. "Jan. 29, 1921. Four American gentlemen were in this cabin when trees fell pinning them to the floor, fire started in stove. Rescued by God and five men from other cabin."[68]

At Cowichan Lake, cruisers working for a Texas company going over the timber limits of the VM&LC heard the wind come up in the hills with a roar, like an approaching battle. Then they heard the trees up the hillside crack, one after another, like machine guns. A few minutes later the storm came down into the big timber that was being cruised. Each gust brought giant trees crashing down with great roars and bringing other trees down with them. The cruisers lost their entire camp and the men spent the night dodging falling Douglas-firs.[69] Old loggers say that never in history had there been such destruction of valuable timber on the Island.

For the first time a seaplane was used to survey the damage done by the wind storm. The plane came from the Jericho Beach Air Station in Vancouver.[70] Alberni forestry officer Robert C. Gritten flew to the interior of the Island around Great Central and Sproat Lakes and over to the Nitinat Valley. In the Nitinat Valley alone, 3000 acres of timber had been destroyed.

More dire predictions in August 1923: if something were not done soon, the forest grove would be gone within the next two years. E. J. Palmer saw the beauty of Cathedral Grove and heard the calls to preserve this treasure; he offered it to the provincial government for a park. His proposition asking for $500,000 to be paid at the end of twenty years with taxes of $10,000 to be paid immediately, did not raise any fire, or interest, within government circles. A few days after his proposition was formally rejected, he gave an option to buy at $800,000 to an American interest,[71] but this too was rejected.[72]

Palmer had more on his mind than Cathedral Grove on November 17, 1923 when a fire broke out in the VL&MC sawmill. At first there seemed little cause for alarm, but the fire spread quickly to engulf the entire mill. Residents of Chemainus stood and watched as their livelihood went up in flames. Some predicted this would be the end of the town. Many of the workers left the community after the fire. Then the good news came in December: the mill would be rebuilt and it would be a "showpiece, costing $3.5 million."[73]

There were rumours Palmer might retire at the end of 1923 and be replaced by Humbird's grandson, John A. Humbird. Palmer had been mill manager for thirty-three years. On Christmas Eve he suffered a

The forest floor carpeted with evergreen sword fern.

AVM PN 468

Top of grade, people facing west, Alberni Highway, *c.* 1922.

AVM PN 1503

1912 Winton car in Cathedral Grove.

AVM PN 4428

Angel Rock, Cameron Lake in 1913.

John A. Humbird, Victoria Lumber & Manufacturing Co. Ltd.

H. R. MacMillan.

Victoria Lumber & Manufacturing Co. Ltd. mill in Chemainus, destroyed by fire in 1923.

BE CAREFUL.

Save Forest Revenue to Develop B.C.

Port Alberni News, July 23, 1919.

stroke and died January 11, 1924.[74] John Humbird took over the management of the mill, but his father, T. J. Humbird, kept a close eye on the business.

Two months later, the managing secretary of the Victoria Chamber of Commerce, George I. Warren, informed his directors the CPR had given notice the logging company that had taken over the forest at Cathedral Grove had decided to begin cutting within the next two months. James O. Cameron, owner of the Cameron Lumber Company in Victoria, predicted the loggers would "clean everything off. Only the stumps will be left."[75]

The Cameron Lumber Company, which was owned and operated by brothers James O. and D. O. Cameron, specialized in making fir cross-arms for telegraph and telephone poles, a growth industry at the time. During the First World War the company also manufactured ammunition boxes.[76]

The dire predictions of the early twenties never came to pass. The trees remained standing and stayed in the hands of the VL&MC as the province got caught up in a mini boom which brought unprecedented growth. The forest industry grew in leaps and bounds. There were now 40,000 men working in the lumber industry in British Columbia. The railways were also making money shipping forest products. H. R. MacMillan turned a small profit on his Export Company selling railway ties to Great Britain. He hired W. J. VanDusen as manager; the two had met in Toronto in 1910, and later, as chief forester, MacMillan had hired VanDusen as district forester of Vancouver. They made an ideal business team; the aggressive MacMillan worked well with the quiet, industrious VanDusen.[77] MacMillan's Export Company seized an opportunity by opening an office in Tokyo when Japan experienced an earthquake and tidal wave that killed 200,000 people and destroyed half a million homes.[78] Japan became one of British Columbia's best customers.

Also during the twenties, (the exact date cannot be confirmed), Frank J. D. Barnjum of Halifax, Nova Scotia, visited Klitsa Lodge, a holiday resort at Sproat Lake near Port Alberni. Barnjum, described as "an energetic little man with grey hair and keen eyes," was one of Canada's foremost advocates of reforestation.

Born in 1858 in Montreal, Barnjum became a millionaire by 1919. He had accumulated his fortune as a merchant with extensive lumbering interests. In 1919, with F. J. Mosely & Company of Boston, he purchased and became president of the MacLeod Pulp Company Limited of Halifax.[79] Barnjum had promoted an embargo on the export of pulpwood to the United States; the many letters he had written to the media about the depletion of Canada's forests had aroused some interest in reforestation.

His rallying cries were "Save the forests," "Spare the trees," and "Preserve our natural heritage."

A self-educated man, Barnjum attended public schools in Montreal until he was thirteen years of age. His first job had been as an office errand boy. In 1923 he retired to devote himself to the conservation of Canada's forests, and he purchased large tracts of forests in various parts of Canada. In British Columbia, in the early thirties, he bought 2,300 acres of giant trees.[80]

After he retired from business, Barnjum set aside half of his fortune for a one-man campaign to conserve the Dominion's fast-vanishing forest resources. Wherever he went, whether to New York, London, Paris, The Hague or Berlin, he talked trees. Sometimes he became disgusted with the cold-blooded indifference of Canadians towards the slaughter of their forests, and in one of these moods he decided to sell his vast holdings and leave the country because he had "no desire to live in a treeless country, a condition which Canada is fast approaching."[81]

What had been a hobby became a passion and then an obsession. He crossed the country many times, urging governments to adopt policies of conservation and reforestation on clearcuts and burnt lands.[82] Between 1920 and 1933 he spent an estimated $50,000 a year trying to awaken public conscience. To administer and protect his timber holdings, he established the Barnjum Forest Foundation.

The owner of Klitsa Lodge, Mrs. Josephine Wark, told Barnjum about local efforts to preserve Cathedral Grove as a park. Mrs. Helen Ford, who researched Sproat Lake extensively and interviewed Josephine Wark many times, said it had been Barnjum who saved the giant trees of Cathedral Grove from logging at this time. Research efforts to validate a connection in this regard have proved fruitless, but Mrs. Ford remains convinced of the authenticity of Barnjum's influence. One could specu-late Barnjum knew E. J. Palmer of VL&MC from meetings of the Cana-dian Forestry Association, and it may have been Barnjum who convinced Palmer to make an offer to the province to preserve the forest for a park. As already stated, this offer was rejected.

In 1924, Barnjum felt he had fought a lost battle, and was about to offer his 450,000 acres of timber, pulp mills, barns, houses and other property "for sale to the first buyer who comes along," when he noticed the political climate had changed in Nova Scotia and offered his name as a candidate in the provincial election. He received the endorsement of Queen's County and served as a Conservative member under Honour-able E. N. Rhodes who swept the Liberals from office after forty years. Barnjum found his plans for action in the Legislature did not materialize, and, disillusioned, resigned after only two years.

Barnjum maintained a beautiful home, "The Gables," at Annapolis Royal, but he spent little time there after his resignation from the Legislature. He began to travel, making several trips to England researching his possible family connections to the Barninghams of Norfolk. The Nova Scotia "lumber king and friend of the trees," died while receiving treatment at the Neuilly Clinic, in Paris, in February 1933. Sadly, the Barnjum Forest Foundation was dissolved, and his heirs sold his timber holdings to forest companies.

Still, the idea of preserving Cathedral Grove for a park remained alive in 1928 when the Qualicum Beach Board of Trade passed a resolution requesting the government and other public organizations reserve the tract of timber as "a memorial of bygone days."[83]

The Qualicum Beach Board of Trade had been formed only two years when the subject of the Cameron Lake timber came up for discussion. In the Board's minute book dated August 8, 1928, realtor Percy H. Buller proposed, and A. N. Fraser seconded, the following resolution, which carried:

> Whereas the finest stand of timber left on Vancouver Island within access to the public is that on the west end of Cameron Lake containing trees from 500 to 600 years old, and whereas, in due course, if steps are not taken to avoid such a tragedy, these trees will be falled, therefore be it resolved that the Qualicum Beach Board of Trade request the government and other public bodies concerned, that this tract, known as Block 35 should be preserved as a memorial of bygone days and of great educational value to all.[84]

The same resolution came before the Courtenay-Comox Board of Trade meeting where a few skeptics doused optimism about the proposal. One businessman considered the lumber industry too strong and it would not do any good to endorse the resolution. For years the Board of Trade had failed to get a reserve around Elk Falls preserved. In moving the resolution be received and filed, Mayor McKenzie questioned what would be done with the trees if they were preserved. After all, he said, "they were mature now and they would only blow down and be a source of trouble and expense to the government."[85]

There was, however, firm support from the Associated Boards of Trade of Vancouver Island. At the annual convention of the Association held in Victoria in 1929, members unanimously endorsed the following resolution which was forwarded to Premier S. F. Tolmie.

> Resolved that this Convention of the Associated Boards of Trade of Vancouver Island again urge the Government to take prompt measures to preserve forever, for the public benefit, the well known stand of timber at Cameron Lake, known as Cathedral Grove.[86]

The Great Depression of the thirties blew away all thoughts of preserving the Grove as people concentrated all their efforts on just surviving.

There were no passionate calls to save the big trees when stomachs were empty and cupboards bare.

The estimated value of one-third (1200 acres) of Block 35 was now $160,000.[87]

A SIGHTING

West Coast Advocate, Port Alberni: June 7, 1934. A white deer seen on several occasions last year by E&N trainmen near Arrowsmith Junction and Cameron Lake, was seen again this week near Cathedral Grove by a local resident returning by motor at night from a trip to the east coast. The animal was fascinated by the car lights and watched them for some time before stalking off into the woods. It was described as being almost pure white from head to tail and what is rather unusual for this time of year, carried a mature set of antlers.

The white deer is a symbol rooted in mythology; it symbolizes light and darkness, sun and storm, and life and death. Stories abound in folklore about white animals. In the United States there are tales of the White Doe of the Roanoke Island,[88] the White Mustang,[89] the White Buffalo, the White Dog of the Iroquois who, in midwinter, in the holiest festival of their theology, was sacrificed to the Great Spirit. A widely known European tradition is that of the white stag, frequently portrayed with golden antlers. In the Alpine area of Slovenia, northwestern Yugoslavia, a white chamois appears in the popular tradition instead of the white stag.[90]

Stories of white animals speak of passion and a quest to control the object of the passion. At this time, within Cathedral Grove, the sighting of the white deer evoked concern regarding the future of the Grove. Could this sighting be a sign good things were about to happen to the forest, or was it a forewarning? Who would eventually control the giant trees? Would the right decision be made regarding its future?

The underside of the Canadian Pacific Railway trestle bridge
on the east side of Cameron Lake.

Chapter Six

TALL TIMBER—CATHEDRAL GROVE

They tell me that I'm getting old!
That all my days are done!
I cannot grow beyond my size
So now my course is run!
They say that I'll be dying soon
A hundred years or so—
And they would hasten my decease
To swell their lucred flow!

Suppose all creatures God has made
Mature, by men were slain,
A sorry world this place would be,
A passioned, youthful reign!
The very men who plot my doom—
Whose property I am—
Mature would die, and, rotting, lie
Unsung by mortal men.

Despite my age, full many a man
Has stood beneath my shade
To drink his fill of deepest joy,
And peace with God has made.
Come! tear me down!
but you will find
That tears are shed for me;
A blasted, blighted, hellish site
Will all your portion be!

PERCY E. WILLS, FEBRUARY 3, 1936

SAFE FROM
THE LOGGER'S AXE

*E*arly in 1936 there were more reports logging operations would be underway shortly in Cathedral Grove. The Port Alberni Board of Trade secretary E. W. Griffiths fired off a letter to the government asking for comment. The Minister of Lands, the Honourable Arthur Wellesley

(Wells) Gray, advised he had no information cutting would begin, but promised to investigate. Gray, born and raised in New Westminster, served as mayor of that city for a period in 1913.[91] He entered provincial politics by winning a by-election on August 25, 1927. He became Minister of Lands in 1933.

The MLA for Alberni and later Comox, Alberni lawyer, L. Arnold Hanna, had persistently urged preservation by the government and often stood on the floor of the House speaking passionately about "the last stand of giant trees." Government members listened respectfully but took no action. Hector Stewart, editor of the *West Coast Advocate* in Port Alberni, expressed his community's feelings on the subject.

> Cathedral Grove must not be logged! It's all very well for our logging friends to say that the trees are past their prime and conky at the top and will soon fall down if they're not cut down, but so long as they are standing, they're worth many times more to the people of Vancouver Island than they ever would bring in the lumber markets of the world. Everyone knows that. And that's one reason why we are not inclined to take too seriously the story that Cathedral Grove is to make sawmill fodder.

> It is inconceivable that any government in its sober senses would be foolhardy enough to commit such a sin against the beauties of nature—more than inconceivable that it would thus dare to act in the face of an aroused public. Mr. Hanna would not then be alone in his single-handed fight to save the Grove. Isn't it about time to suppress once and for all this hardy annual; the bugaboo about logging Cathedral Grove? The Pattullo government can make a good fellow of itself by taking the necessary action now, either by outright purchase or by trading for some other government owned timber tract less desirable from a scenic stand point and the sooner it's done the better—for the government knows and the loggers know and the public know, that CATHEDRAL GROVE MUST NOT BE LOGGED![92]

Shortly after this editorial appeared, Wells Gray advised the Port Alberni Board of Trade he would make every effort to save the Grove, and on his own initiative, he would take steps to preserve the natural beauty of Little Qualicum Falls and Cameron Lake.[93]

W. M. Neal, vice-president of the CPR, president of the Esquimalt & Nanaimo Railway, and a member of the company's advisory committee in charge of the administration of its natural resources, sent an intercompany letter to D. C. Coleman, also a CPR vice-president. Knowing the company's vested interest in the area and in tourism, Neal mentioned Wells Gray's intervention on behalf of the Grove. The CPR still owned hundreds of acres of timber from the original E&N Land Grant. The CPR asked Humbird if he would be willing to negotiate, but Humbird declined to name a figure, stating that while his company had no concrete plan to offer, "they would be glad to consider any reasonable suggestion." He observed that during the past thirteen years every Minister of Lands and every Chief Forester had advanced the proposition, but no plan had ever been considered feasible. Neal advised he would talk to Humbird personally when next on Vancouver Island with the hope of establishing a reasonable price.[94]

Wells Gray, hearing nothing further from the CPR, wrote again on March 17, 1937, refreshing the memory of earlier discussions with D. C. Coleman and enclosing a letter he had received from the Local Council of Women in Victoria. He also enclosed letters of support from Lord Tweedsmuir, the Governor General of Canada, and Ernest H. Hutchinson, the Secretary of State for the State of Washington. Lord Tweedsmuir wrote:

> Never have I seen a place so filled with natural beauties as Vancouver Island. I want to appeal to you citizens to realize the value of your heritage and to preserve it. It is easy even in a great country like this to destroy it. The richness of the flora and fauna is not inexhaustible. If you allow careless spoliation: if you allow your game laws to be so badly managed as to destroy the fauna, you kill the goose that lays the golden eggs. Take care you do not let the wonderful natural growth of Vancouver Island disappear through carelessness—see that you protect that growth for the future good of your island. You have a treasure house that is worth the saving.[95]

An editorial in the *Cowichan Leader* of Duncan indicated the VL&MC would be willing to sell its holdings at Cathedral Grove to the government or enter an exchange for another tract elsewhere. On March 4, 1936, Wells Gray advised the Victoria and Island Publicity Bureau negotiations were being carried out to save the Grove.[96]

Once again, MLA Arnold Hanna kept up the pressure on the Patullo government by warning of the dire consequences should the effort to save the Grove fail. "No axe or saw has yet touched Cathedral Grove and I would like to tell the Minister of Lands that if this area of timber is not saved for posterity as a timber reserve, this government may as well close up."[97]

Roland E. Brinckman, tongue-in-cheek, submitted a poem about the Grove to the *West Coast Advocate*, in Port Alberni:

> Wat's all this talk of Cathedral Grove?
> Why shouldn't we cut it down?
> What right have people who beauty love
> To shake their heads and frown?
> Why shouldn't we spoil the country-side?
> Why shouldn't we chop and slash?
> Who in mere landscape would take a pride,
> If it couldn't be turned into cash.
>
> Think of the packing-cases new:
> Think of the sashes and doors:
> Think of the shiplap and V-joint too:
> Think of the two-by-fours.

MLA L. Arnold Hanna,
Liberal, 1928-1933.

A. Wells Gray.

Angel Rock.   COURTESY AARON VISSIER

AVM PN 658

Virgin Douglas-fir in Cathedral Grove, 1924.

MLA James Mowat,
Liberal, 1941-1952.

H. R. MacMillan
saw the huge
potential of
B.C. forests and
forest products.

AVM PN 2237

There ain't no money in Beauty, boys,
And money's our god, that's flat:
For Beauty only the Soul enjoys
And the Soul—my gawd—what's that?

Within two years, from 1934 to 1936, the value of the Grove increased to $210,000.[98]

In July 1936, Wells Gray arranged to submit a proposal on the preservation of Cathedral Grove to a committee composed of a representative of the Department of Lands and a representative of the Canadian Pacific Railway.[99] Gray had discussed with the federal government the possibility of the Canadian Parks Branch taking over some of B.C.'s larger parks, but the federal government seemed chiefly interested in Mount Robson Park and the possibility of a new park on the west coast of Vancouver Island. A few years before, the Department of the Interior inspected various areas on the west coast with the idea of establishing a "seaside national park." The choice then lay between Carmanah Beach and Long Beach.[100] Victoria preferred Carmanah over Long Beach. The Long Beach National Park remained just a proposition as long as the road from Alberni to the west coast awaited development.[101]

Gray contacted Humbird in April of 1937 to seek some accommodation regarding the Grove. He suggested two methods, cash or timber exchange.

> I do not know whether the Government has at its disposal at the present time a stand of timber which would be suitable for the purpose, but it is possible that such timber may be found within the Railway Belt, and in that case assistance may be obtained from the Canadian Pacific Railway Company. Such a plan would be more acceptable to the Government than payment in cash.[102]

Humbird replied:

> Suggested trade would be preferable, as far as we are concerned, to receiving cash for the timber. In such a trade we would, of course, expect that you would take into consideration in addition to quantity, the quality and comparable logging costs. We would naturally prefer timber which could be made available to our operation at Chemainus.[103]

A deal appeared possible if the CPR could be convinced to contribute to the scheme. Negotiations between all parties continued during the summer. In the fall, the CPR made it clear it would not be interested in making any "substantial contribution either in money or timber to enable the Grove to be set aside as desired"[104] until a plan had been fully developed. The railway company felt it had no obligation to contribute and considered if it did participate in the proposed park, then it should be in conjunction with the VL&MC.

The H. R. MacMillan Export Company, after ten years in business, now had a share in Chehalis Logging Company and owned and operated the

Canadian White Pine Company Limited, the H. R. MacMillan Log Company, a railway tie division, the Canadian Transport Company, and the Victoria and Vancouver Stevedoring Company. H. R. MacMillan had spread his wings and had regular customers and agents around the globe. Montague Meyer had earlier sold out his interest to MacMillan.

MacMillan received some unwanted competition in the export market business for the first time, when in 1935, a consortium headed by president John Humbird of the VL&MC, established Seaboard Lumber Sales and Seaboard Shipping.[105] MacMillan reacted to this competition by buying several companies, including the Vancouver Plywood plant and the Alberni Pacific Lumber Company (APL) of Port Alberni. Denny, Mott & Dickson Ltd., of London, England, sold the APL sawmill and timber holdings in the valley of Stamp and Ash Rivers for an estimated $4 million. VanDusen, a close associate of MacMillan, was named vice-president of the new company. MacMillan had started the acquisition of a huge empire of timber, a wise move considering the timber shortage that followed. From 1935 to 1939 MacMillan's Alberni sawmill logged its best stands of timber and now cut high on the mountainsides.

Wells Gray continued his pressure on the CPR to preserve the Grove as a tourist park. In the spring of 1939, he travelled east and met with railway officials. Meantime, travel through the Grove became easier when the government allocated money to "hard-surface" the road.[106]

By the fall of 1939, world leaders were pleading for peace in Europe. All wood operations in the Central Island area were closed down under order of the Forestry Department because of severe fire hazards. No one could enter the woods unless by special permit. Fishermen could only fish on lakes that could be reached by public highway. Even prospectors waited impatiently for rain so they could go back into the hills. Loggers took advantage of the opportunity to go to "town"—nearly all were headed for Nanaimo. A steady stream of buses, trains, and taxis wound their way through the Grove and Cameron Valley.

Water and ice pattern a maple leaf.

Chapter Seven

Discoveries: IV

within the limits of this paper
i can run raindrops
in vermeil ditches
find a leaf large as the coast
squeeze out its wet pungency
settle it in bureau drawers
too weak to contain its fragrance
follow its message through my room
through my mind
take in a forest on my simplest terms
in the middle of my madness am more sane
than all the sombre rules of art

FLORENCE MCNEIL, *Emily*

THREATS AND ENDORSEMENTS

*A*ll thoughts of preserving the small grove of trees were forgotten when Canada declared war in September 1939. Immediately, all resources were mobilized into the war effort. The forest industry in British Columbia entered a new period of growth when the Timber Control Board of Great Britain began importing wood to build training camps and evacuation centres.[107] Sawmill owners were worried; shipping had become a problem as lumber piled up in yards and docks. All lumber shipments from British Columbia had stopped after a ship carrying lumber was torpedoed off the California coast.[108] Orders were plentiful but there was no way to get the lumber to its destination.[109] MacMillan proposed it be transported to the east coast for shipment, thus reducing the time it would take to ship through the Panama Canal. An agreement reached in March 1940 with the CPR and Canadian National Railways permitted lumber to be shipped east by rail.

Even the last of the old sailing ships in the Canadian timber trade, the *Vigilant*, launched in 1919, was recruited into service after being purchased by the Canadian Transport Company Ltd., the shipping arm of

H. R. MacMillan Export Company, and renamed *City of Alberni*. Loaded with 1.6 million board feet of lumber, she travelled to Australia in the summer of 1940. The twenty-year-old five-masted topsail schooner managed to dodge enemy ships and even weathered a hurricane while travelling a distance of 6800 miles from Vancouver to Sydney in eighty days. After the third trip, the proud ship sadly ended her days on a reef.[110]

Into the forties, MacMillan continued his acquisition spree, buying up E&N Railway company timber land that had passed into other hands during the Depression and was now on the market. He also bought the Thomsen & Clark Timber Company of Courtenay for its tax benefit; he purchased the Shawnigan Lake Lumber Company for its timber holdings, and from the Canadian Robert Dollar Company he acquired 35,000 acres of timber north of Nanaimo and formed the Northwest Bay Logging Company. In addition, he built a plywood mill in Port Alberni to complement his Vancouver operation. Despite MacMillan's busy schedule, he managed to find time to relax either on his converted minesweeper *Marijean*, named for his two daughters, or on his thousand-acre hobby farm near Qualicum, where he raised cattle, sheep, pigs, and turkeys.

The Department of Highways continued to improve the highway through the Grove and around Cameron Lake, which had become a bottleneck for traffic. In the summer of 1940 the road was straightened somewhat when a portion of the rock face, known locally as Angel Rock, was bulldozed to allow a 10 per cent curve at the strategic corner.[111] A sign posted at the dangerous corner warned drivers to "Honk your horn," before navigating the turn. For years, the Albernis' Board of Trade and community organizations had repeatedly complained to the Minister of Public Works about this dangerous portion of the highway. An added inducement for government improvements at this time could have been the possibility of a large pulp mill being located in Port Alberni. The widening of the highway would then be imperative.

Meanwhile, Wells Gray, under an Order-in-Council, suspended provisions in the Forest Act related to the sale of Crown timber for forest products that were urgently needed for war purposes. He also suspended conditions on existing timber sales, conditions that were curtailing production of urgently needed materials.[112] Logging and lumbering were now officially classified as essential war industries.

Alarm bells rang in the Albernis and in neighbouring communities when logging operations began close to the Grove in March 1940. The Port Alberni and Alberni District Boards of Trade and city councils were unanimous in their cry for preservation. All were reassured by Wells Gray, who, knowing of the logging, said, "as far as the government is aware there is no intention of logging Cathedral Grove."[113] Residents backed their municipal leaders' stand with the warning, "the Grove must not be touched or endangered." A petition for the preservation of Cathedral Grove as a park site originated with the Port Alberni council and began to circulate among Island communities.

Although the pressure was mounting to preserve Cathedral Grove, two other parks in the same area were designated. On December 20, 1940, the provincial government announced the establishment of new parks at nearby Little Qualicum Falls and Englishman River Falls.[114] Both of these spectacular waterfalls were deep in the forests south and east of Cathedral Grove.

Following the retirement of MLA Arnold Hanna to his law practice in Port Alberni in 1941, the lobbying for the Grove fell into the hands of the new Alberni MLA James Mowat, a Port Alberni shoe-store owner. Before long, Mowat knocked on the door of Wells Gray asking for assurances something would be done to preserve the Grove. Gray could give no such assurances.

At a Port Alberni and District Board of Trade meeting in the Somass Hotel, on March 12, 1941, the cry again echoed among delegates, "Save Cathedral Grove!" Each year, a new executive faced the same problem of how to deal with the threat posed by logging operations taking place close to the Grove. Each year, another protest was forwarded to Victoria describing "the grandest scenic tourist asset in British Columbia."[115]

In July 1942, at a meeting of the Tourist Association of the Pacific Coast held in the Hotel Vancouver, delegates, after discussing Cathedral Grove, filed a protest with the provincial government and called for its preservation.[116] The Vancouver Board of Trade strongly endorsed the move and with other boards on the Lower Mainland followed suit. Nanaimo Mayor Harrison wholeheartedly gave his support; he promised to speak with the Island Boards of Trade and seek their participation in support of preservation.

One week later, the B.C. Natural Resources Conservation League was formed to protect the natural resources of the province, including scenic spots such as Cathedral Grove. Frank Burd, president of the Vancouver *Daily Province* became honourary president with the Honourable H. H. Stevens as president.[117] With a newspaperman at the helm and with the support of newspapers in the province, the organization began awakening public opinion towards conservation of the Grove. The Vancouver *Daily Province* in August quoted John Humbird as saying: "Under ordinary conditions we would take the Cathedral Grove timber in our stride and cut it when it served our purpose best. Off hand I can't say just when that time might be. But I recognize that because of the scenic beauty of the Cameron Lake forest, we should deal with it as a special case, and are willing to do so." Humbird said his company would be willing to make a

Windfalls float on the edge of Cameron Lake.

Lichen on the branches.

Shaggy mane mushrooms.

A view of Cameron River which begins at Labour Day Lake,
24 kms southeast of the park.

trade with the provincial government for timber in some other area equivalent to what he would be losing by surrendering control of Cathedral Grove to the Province.

Now that the media had come on side, public opinion developed in favour of preserving the Grove. The tall timbers of Cameron Lake seemed to be on everyone's mind. Port Alberni Mayor Mike Hamilton decided there had been enough talk and it was time everyone knew if the Grove would be logged or not. He sent the following telegram to B.C.'s Chief Forester, C. D. Orchard: "Reports indicate you are opposed to preservation of Cathedral Grove. Be advised people here are very determined on its preservation."[118]

One old-timer from Sproat Lake, Alex Sproat, the son of Gilbert Malcolm Sproat, (the representative of the Anderson Company, which built and operated an export sawmill in Alberni from 1860-64), had his own version of earlier events related to Cathedral Grove which he wrote in a letter to Irving Wilson, editor of the *West Coast Advocate* in Port Alberni.

At the time the Chemainus mill acquired this tract—Henry Croft, brother-in-law of James Dunsmuir—the E&N Railway market price for land and timber was $1 an acre. The taxes were then, and for a long period, very low. This timber was not logged at the time it should have been, when in its prime, owing to the intervention of R. M. Marpole, Executive Agent of the CPR Mr. Marpole had the idea it was an added attraction to lure tourists over their main line to the Island railroad. I heard him remark on the train one midday as it slowly climbed up to and around the S curves, seemingly level with this timber, "What a grand sight." You can understand this statement clearer from the fact that the railroad was built primarily for tourists, thus accounting for the steep grades and curves, so that passengers could linger longer with their eyes on attractive spots.

Every timberman knows that the timber now is not merchantable; no one would fall the timber for logs if times were normal. It is badly stained, wind-shaken, very old. It looks grand as long as it stands up to anyone passing rapidly through and should be by all means left there for public pleasure as long as it remains standing. Mr. Humbird, of course, knows all this. So does the Minister. Perhaps Mr. Humbird is pushing the general public to demand now that the Government trade a good merchantable tract in exchange.

The Minister knows the timber is not suitable for lumber and evidently is in no hurry to show his hand in a poker game whereby financially the lumber baron is bound to win. No matter what the Government does, I know that one difficulty the Department faces, is to furnish a tract suitable to the Chemainus interests from available Government timber. There has been, from the beginning, a towering exploitation of public land in all the transactions connected with the E&N railway grant. The CPR bought the road and paid for it in CPR stock, now worth very little. This railway, for years, has been by far the best paying road on the CPR system, yet they cannot run a passenger train on time. But you do right, old man, to insist the minister get this matter settled quickly.

ALEX SPROAT

Sproat's letter came at a time when the Albernis were experiencing poor rail passenger service. The continued late arrival of the evening train raised the ire of businessmen, postal staff, and residents alike. Trains left with practically no passengers, yet at the same time buses leaving were filled to capacity. Everyone agreed the train schedule should be changed to meet the ferry service to Vancouver.

Once again, the Victoria Local Council of Women took up the cause as it had done previously in 1937. Only this time, the group wrote directly to the CPR Vice-President of Western Lines, W. A. Mather. Convenor of the Local Council of Women on National Recreation and Natural Resources, Elizabeth C. MacKenzie, wrote in her letter dated November 12, 1942 about the importance of maintaining Cathedral Grove as a monument to those who died in war.[119] She argued:

> For the future well being of the Island, and in the interests of the Company in general, we do urge that the Company consider the making of a gift to the Government for the benefit of the people, of those timber lands in their possession bordering on the highway on the south of Cameron Lake, as far East as the entrance to little Qualicum Falls. The timber values involved in this road strip on Cameron Lake are small.

> Should the Government be successful in its efforts to effect an exchange of timber with the owners of the big timber west of the Lake, for an area through which the highway runs, sufficient to maintain the fine forest effect which is so worthy of preservation, then, with the strips of timber lands bordering the Lake, the conservation of a great scenic asset would be assured and a matter which has been before the public for some twenty-five years or more, through successive administrations, brought to a successful conclusion.

MacKenzie appealed to the CPR's sensitivity for "those lads who so recently loved to camp, swim and climb in this lovely place, but who have given their lives on land, sea and in the air, for our freedom."

The forest industry growth in the early forties had been such that both industry and government began to recognize and decry the unregulated exploitation of the valuable resource and looked for ways to develop a system based on sustained yield. The question was asked, could forests be considered a renewable resource as agricultural crops were? To find out, the provincial government, in 1943, appointed Chief Justice Gordon Sloan of the B.C. Supreme Court to investigate and report back on whether it was possible to operate the forest industry on a continuous production basis. The Sloan Report had an impact on every section of the industry and showed clearly that a perpetual yield was essential to the industry and to the B.C. economy. Tree Farm Licences were subsequently established and companies were assured there would be enough timber to allow them to proceed with mill expansions.

What happened in the forests now had become important in the lives of every British Columbian. When a few Grove trees fell by the highway and some individuals saw an opportunity for some easy firewood, members of the Alberni Board of Trade protested vehemently: no trees should be cut until the provincial government had taken the necessary steps to protect the Grove. Premier John Hart claimed no trees were being cut down, and he added, "Negotiations are going on, but these things take time."[120] The government clearly understood the sensitive nature of the issue: the citizens of British Columbia wanted this grove of trees protected. Premier John Hart went one step further in April 1944 by declaring Cathedral Grove would not be cut by loggers. This announcement by the Premier would have been music to the ears of Wells Gray, who had tried so hard to remove the obstacles that prevented the preservation of the Grove. Only weeks later, Gray died of a fatal heart attack May 7, 1944. The estimated value of the Grove had risen since 1936 to $585,000.[121]

A young hemlock growing out of a decayed nurse log.

Arbutus tree bark.

Chapter Eight

PRAYER OF THE FOREST

Man! I am the heat of your hearth against
    the cold winter nights;
I am the friendly shade against the
    burning summer sun.
I am the builder of your home, the board
    of your table.
I am the bed that holds your slumbers and
    the wood from which
You fashion your ships.
I am the shaft of your hoe and the door to
    your chamber.
I am your cradle and your coffin.
I am the bread of goodness and the flower
    of beauty.
Hear my prayer and destroy me not.

AUTHOR UNKNOWN

THE GIFT

*I*n 1944, MacMillan shocked the industry when he announced his company had become managing agents for the VL&MC. The Humbird family had in fact sold the VL&MC to E. P. Taylor, a Toronto financier with interests in Massey-Harris, later known as Massey-Ferguson, manufacturers of agricultural implements. The name of the sawmill was changed to Victoria Lumber Company (VLC). MacMillan had persuaded his friend Taylor there were great opportunities within the British Columbia forest industry. If Taylor purchased the VL&MC, he, MacMillan, would "take it off his hands after a suitable interval."[122] MacMillan needed the company's large timber holdings. Earlier when Humbird let it be known he wanted to sell the mill, he said he would never sell to H. R. MacMillan. Humbird's dislike of MacMillan was deep-rooted and stemmed from his abrupt departure from the VL&MC. They were also business rivals in the export market. Humbird accepted Taylor's $8 million offer. The announcement of the sale came in April 1944, and by June it was further announced the H. R. MacMillan Export Company would manage the mill for a fee of $250,000 a year.[123]

The government immediately opened negotiations with the new owners of Cathedral Grove. The premier believed an arrangement could be made "without delay"[124] to exchange the Grove for another merchantable stand under government control. In September 1944, Premier Hart personally inspected the Grove with his chief forester, C. D. Orchard. For several hours they tramped through the forest and looked over the stands of timber along Cameron Lake.[125]

In a document dated November 20, 1944, from MacMillan to Premier John Hart regarding Cathedral Grove Park, MacMillan stated he had arranged with E. P. Taylor, president of VLC, "that he leave this matter in my hands." MacMillan added:

> We sympathize with your desire that this unique tract of old-growth Douglas-fir timber on the Trans-Canada highway should be preserved in perpetuity as a park for the benefit of the public. Therefore, although this tract of timber is the most valuable for its size in the holdings of the Victoria Lumber Company because of the high quality of the timber and its situation 15 miles from salt water and on a good highway, the Company authorises me to made a gift of the tract of about 330 acres. This area includes the large trees in which the public is interested, and is large enough to fill all the requirements of a park, being about one-half the size of the forested portion of Stanley Park.[126]

MacMillan promised to obtain approval for the land transfer from the company shareholders. Should they disapprove, he assured no trees would fall within the proposed park prior to April 15, 1956 when the bonds were paid off and the park title transferred to the government. In return, MacMillan asked that taxes paid on the land since it was acquired from the E&N Railway be repaid to the VLC. The company also wanted to retain its right-of-way through the park when it would begin logging the remaining timber in the adjoining new boundaries of Block 35 in a few years' time.

Premier Hart quickly responded to MacMillan's generous offer, thanking him and accepting the gift on behalf of the people of British Columbia. "Believe me when I say that your action enables the Government to preserve for posterity and develop for the benefit of the public a delightful park land which should bring a large measure of recreation and enjoyment not only to British Columbians but thousands of visitors to this Province."[127]

Letters of congratulations flowed into MacMillan's office. S. K. Murray of British Columbia Packers Ltd. commended him for his "magnanimous act." He also wrote, "The Good Book says 'It is more blessed to give than to receive . . .' When you were in the East and I sent along clippings with reference to Cathedral Grove, it never occurred to me that the day would dawn when you would be the donor of this wonderful property to the public." MacMillan's association with B.C. Packers went back to the early thirties, when the fish-packing company added his name to its board of directors. He became president in 1933 at a time when the fishing industry was in financial trouble. MacMillan put the company into the black by consolidating its plants and slashing overhead. He stepped down in 1941.[128]

Other words of praise came from the Bishop of British Columbia, Harold E. Sexton. He suggested the new park be named "MacMillan Park."

The Vancouver Local Council of Women thanked him for his "generous presentation of Cathedral Grove."

Lawyer Ghent Davis reminisced about driving through Cathedral Grove en route to his summer place on Sproat Lake, near Alberni. "I have often thought it would be too bad when it was logged as it seemed certain it would be, so that it was with a great deal of pleasure that I read in the paper of your very wonderful gift to the province. It will certainly mean a great deal to a very large number of people."

Gerald E. Wellburn of Shawnigan Lake Lumber Co. Ltd. wrote to MacMillan's secretary, Miss Dorothy Dee, commenting:

Many a time I have stopped my car at Cathedral Grove, and walked around to pay my respects to these grand old trees, and on several occasions (before gas rationing) I have taken parties of visitors especially to see this truly fine forest. I know of no more beautiful or inspiring sight, than to see the sun shining through these tall trees, and I am personally delighted that Mr. MacMillan has made it possible to preserve the grove for those coming after us.

The Canadian Forestry Association, B.C. branch president, W. F. Stewart, wrote on behalf of his association, "Future generations will be reminded of your generosity in dedicating the Grove to their use. Our Association is proud of the notable contribution you have made to the stability of forestry enterprise in British Columbia."

Not only had MacMillan donated the thirty acres of the Cathedral Grove trees, but to protect the timber he also had given an additional 302 acres surrounding the area. The 332 acres included the northerly portion known as Block 35 which contained two groves of very large trees. The property, with approximately 25,000,000 million board feet of timber, also had 700 yards of frontage on Cameron Lake, plus the Cameron River streams which flowed into the lake. The land on either side of the highway extended to the bridge across the river. Beyond this point, MacMillan retained logging interests.

While everyone in the province, it seemed, had congratulated MacMillan and Premier Hart for reaching an agreement over the park, a Port

From Certificate No. 22369-N

THE GOVERNMENT OF
THE PROVINCE OF BRITISH COLUMBIA

No. 36429-N

Certificate of Indefeasible Title

Date of Application for registration, the___9th___day of___July at 10.20 a.m.___, 19 45

Register, Vol.___146___

This is to certify that HIS MAJESTY THE KING in the right of the Province of British Columbia, In Trust, D.D. 36429-N,

___is___ *absolutely and indefeasibly entitled in fee-simple, subject to such charges, liens, and interests as are notified by endorsement hereon, and subject to the conditions, exceptions, and reservations set out hereon, to* ___that___

piece of land situate in the___ Nanaimo Assessment District

and Province of British Columbia, and more particularly known and described as:— That part of Block thirty-five (35), ALBERNI DISTRICT, Plan 691-K, containing three hundred and thirty-seven (337) acres, more or less, as shown outlined in red on Plan

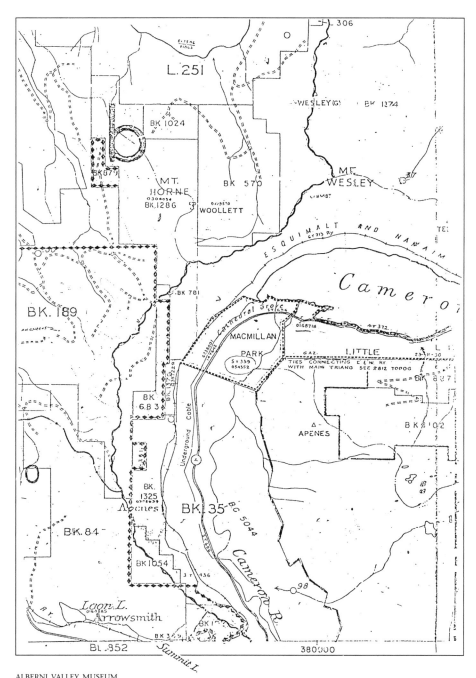

ALBERNI VALLEY MUSEUM

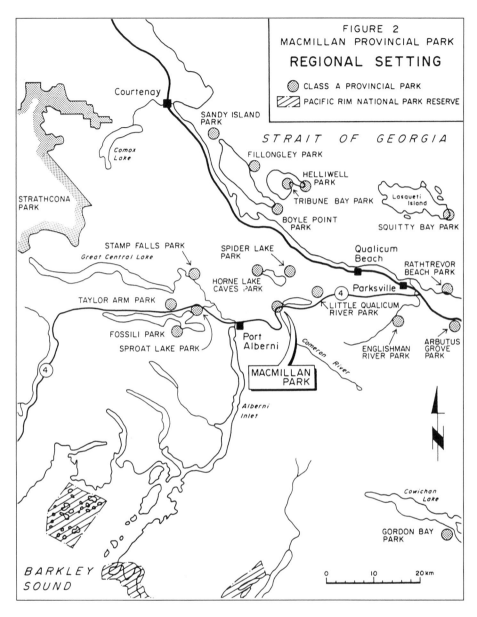

FIGURE 2
MACMILLAN PROVINCIAL PARK
REGIONAL SETTING

CLASS A PROVINCIAL PARK
PACIFIC RIM NATIONAL PARK RESERVE

Courtenay

SANDY ISLAND
PARK

STRAIT   OF   GEORGIA

*Comox
Lake*

FILLONGLEY PARK

HELLIWELL
PARK

STRATHCONA
PARK

*Lasqueti
Island*

TRIBUNE BAY PARK

BOYLE POINT
PARK

SQUITTY BAY PARK

STAMP FALLS PARK
Great Central Lake

SPIDER LAKE
PARK

Qualicum
Beach

RATHTREVOR
BEACH PARK

TAYLOR ARM PARK

HORNE LAKE
CAVES PARK

4   Parksville

LITTLE QUALICUM
RIVER PARK

FOSSILI PARK

Port
Alberni

SPROAT LAKE PARK

ENGLISHMAN
RIVER PARK

ARBUTUS
GROVE
PARK

4

MACMILLAN
PARK

Cameron   River

*Alberni
Inlet*

*Cowichan
Lake*

GORDON BAY
PARK

N

*BARKLEY
SOUND*

0   10   20 km

MAPS COURTESY B.C. PARKS

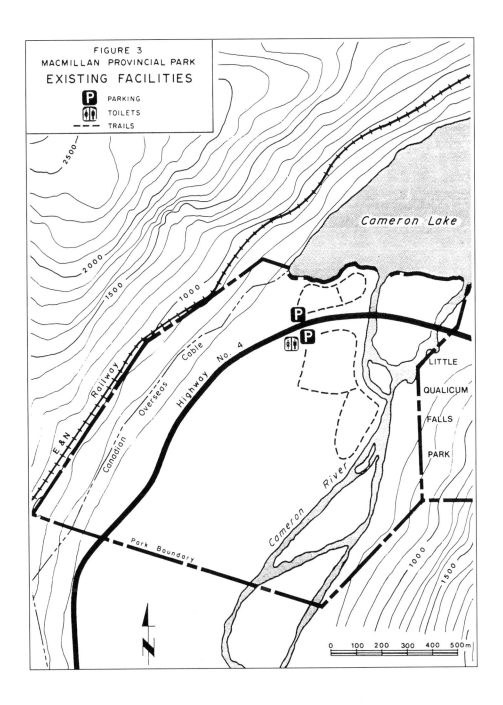

FIGURE 3
MACMILLAN PROVINCIAL PARK
EXISTING FACILITIES

P   PARKING
     TOILETS
- - TRAILS

Cameron Lake

LITTLE
QUALICUM
FALLS
PARK

E & N
Railway
Canadian Overseas Cable
Highway No. 4
Cameron River
Park Boundary

2500
2000
1500
1000
1000
1500

0 100 200 300 400 500m

85

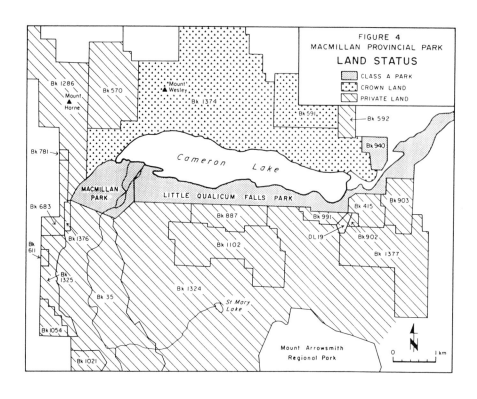

FIGURE 4
MACMILLAN PROVINCIAL PARK
LAND STATUS

CLASS A PARK
CROWN LAND
PRIVATE LAND

Bk 1286
Mount
Horne
Bk 570
Mount
Wesley
Bk 1374
Bk 591
Bk 592
Bk 781
Cameron Lake
Bk 940
MACMILLAN PARK
LITTLE QUALICUM FALLS PARK
Bk 903
Bk 683
Bk 887
Bk 991
Bk 415
Bk 1376
DL 19
Bk 902
Bk 611
Bk 1102
Bk 1377
Bk 1325
Bk 35
Bk 1324
St Mary Lake
Bk 1054
Mount Arrowsmith
Regional Park
Bk 1021
0   1 km

86

Douglas-fir saplings reach for the light.

Alberni newspaper editorial remembered that another participant, Wells Gray, deserved credit in the long battle to save the forest.

> Thanks must be accorded Mr. H. R. MacMillan for his generous gift. . . . For years residents of this district have fought to retain this famous stand of timber, through successive governments and now, instead of having to purchase it or make an exchange the well known industrialist makes a presentation of it to the government. The late Wells Gray, who for many years held down the portfolio of Minister of Lands, promised time and again that it would not be sold or cut down by loggers, but he passed on before his ambition could be realized.

Should the park be named for the donor? Premier Hart thought so. MacMillan, replying to Hart's suggestion, wrote: "Naturally it is likely that the name Cathedral Grove will continue to be used by the public as being an appropriate and widely understood term, which I would not like to see dropped. If you feel it appropriate that my name should be used for the park, I would consider myself honoured."[129]

In December 1944, the Premier announced the new name for Cathedral Grove would be MacMillan Park, in honour of the donor. This announcement touched off a bit of nostalgia for the old name in the Albernis, as evidenced by an editorial December 28, 1944.

> Re Cathedral Grove: It will not, however, become generally known as MacMillan Park. Its main attraction is Cathedral Grove, known the length and breadth of the North American continent and visited annually by hundreds of tourists. To them, its awe-inspiring beauty, its cathedral-like spires of the tall trees from which it derived its name, will never die. It is, and always will be, Cathedral Grove, and it is up to the residents of Vancouver Island to see it remains Cathedral Grove and continually advertised as such. Cathedral Grove is one of the last large stands of timber traversed by a highway and its setting aside as a park is the result of years of agitation. Surely no one can even hope that its name would be changed.

Just as the news of the new park became known, the provincial government announced the construction of a modern highway for the entire length of Vancouver Island as a post-war construction project. The government's first priority was to improve the highway through the Grove. A thirty-foot road would follow the present route as closely as possible and there would be a twenty-five-foot strip on either side of the road cleared of all debris. The number of trees to be cut down within the park would be kept down to forty. Another seventy-three would be cut in Block 35, ensuring safe passage for the public through the park area. The public was assured many of these trees were dead or green firs.[130]

As promised, in 1946, MacMillan purchased Taylor's Victoria Lumber Company by an exchange of shares. MacMillan later reflected this turned out to be one of his better deals. "We have logged it continuously since you (Taylor) bought it, and I am told by our experts that we will still be logging it after the year 2000."[131] E. P. Taylor established B.C. Forest Products Ltd. and began buying up several small sawmills and timber; included in his purchase was the Cameron Lumber Company in Victoria. MacMillan loaned one of his senior executives to his friend to manage the new company, and they agreed that H. R. MacMillan Export Co. would be the exclusive sales agent. This arrangement worked until 1953 when the contract was terminated by mutual consent.[132]

The CPR added another gift to the MacMillan legacy: 839 acres along the shores of Cameron Lake, connecting MacMillan Park with Little Qualicum Falls Park to the east. Premier Hart received the offer in August 1947 from Mr. J. E. McMullen, chairman of the B.C. Sub-Committee, Department of Natural Resources of the E&N Railway.[133] Hart commented when accepting the gift: "It is indeed a most public-spirited action that the officials of the E&N Railway Company have taken." Between MacMillan Park and Little Qualicum Falls, the new strip of parkland contained approximately 1,330 acres of forest, rivers and lakes.

Following the release of the Justice Gordon Sloan report, in 1947 the Forest Act was amended and the province divided into Tree Farm Licences (TFL), or Forest Management Licences. Although Sloan never mentioned TFLs, his observations clearly showed that perpetual yield from productive forests was essential to the B.C. economy. The government had taken the first step towards establishing a permanent forest industry. The old methods so prevalent in the early forest industry, would be no more. Now forest companies would be held responsible for the land entrusted in their care.

MacMillan Park (Cathedral Grove) was officially declared a provincial park on February 25, 1947.

In a series of mergers in the fifties, the H. R. MacMillan Export Co. Ltd. merged with Bloedel, Stewart & Welch Ltd., then later with Powell River Limited, emerging in the sixties as MacMillan Bloedel Limited, now popularly known as MB or MacBlo. MacMillan retired as chairman of the board in 1955 and as honourary chairman in 1961; he remained a member of the executive committee until 1969 and a director until 1970.

H. R. MacMillan had a crusty exterior which disguised the generosity of the inner man, a philosopher and philanthropist who gave $13.2 million to the University of British Columbia and gave the city of Vancouver $3.5 million for the H. R. MacMillan Planetarium. In 1971, he was invested as a Companion of the Order of Canada, the nation's highest award to citizens. MacMillan died in 1976.

Sunlight filters through branches and bridge handrail across Highway 4.

Chapter Nine

THE PARK, THE PEOPLE

*O*n the eve of the fiftieth Anniversary of the designation of Mac-Millan Park (Cathedral Grove), age and disease, combined with increased public usage, have added stress to the ecosystem of the park. Shortly after the announcement of the gift, trees were logged to make way for the new Highway 4, and Angel Rock, which had been such an impediment to early road construction and which had hung precariously over the roadway for years, came crashing down following a winter gale. Eventually the rough edges were trimmed off and the corner widened to make passage easier for large trucks.

Cameron Lake Chalet, which had been the centre of much of the social life of the Central Island area, was leased to a succession of landlords with various plans for the property. The Chalet was destroyed by fire in 1966. Today little remains of what was once a proud and prosperous tourist destination. While local and visiting families can still enjoy the excellent beach facility, Cameron Lake no longer has the world-class reputation it enjoyed when the Chalet was in operation.

There were also changes within the parks system. Until the late forties the provincial park system in British Columbia had been administered by the forest service. Most of the province's parks were large and within scenic mountain settings. In the past, advertising campaigns were designed to attract settlers and investment income into the west. But in the forties, this philosophy changed. The parks were no longer regarded primarily as recreation showplaces; now a new multiple-use philosophy embraced commercial development.[134] Guidelines established by the Park Act classified provincial parks as being either Class "A" or Class "B." Under the former, no commercial or industrial exploitation would be permissible. The latter permitted other resource use as long as it did not detract from the recreational potential of the park. MacMillan Park is a Class "A" park.

In 1948 a special division of government was created to take over parks administration from the forest service; the Grove now fell under the jurisdiction of the Parks Branch of the Department of Recreation and Conservation.

Fire is a word dreaded by loggers, foresters, and park wardens alike. In August 1972 the horror Fletcher warned of so many years before became a reality when vandals set fire to a seven-hundred-year-old redcedar tree. The tree's dimensions were awesome: fifteen feet in diameter, its huge trunk had risen sixty feet before branching into four limbs that soared another two hundred feet. It had been one of the show-trees of the forest. A trail had been cleared so visitors could walk from the highway to see and touch this giant that had started its life about the time of the Magna Carta. Age had hollowed out its trunk, and a crack near the base had opened a hole to its heart. Evidence showed it was here the fire had been deliberately set.[135] The charred remains were left broken on the forest floor—in a furrow dug by the tree's own impact when felled by foresters unable to extinguish the flames—perhaps to serve as a lasting reminder of the ever-present danger of fire in the forest.

This may have been the first time vandals had caused a fire in the Grove, but it was not the first forest fire. Research has shown fire also swept through the park about eight hundred years ago. The Douglas-fir is a fire-dependent species. The trees today resulted from that fire. By the time the next fire occurred five hundred years later, the trees had reached maturity and had developed a thick protective outer bark.

In 1973, a University of British Columbia botanist, Dr. Vladimir Krajina, a member of the British Columbia Ecological Reserves Committee (BCERA), said the fire of 1850 had left the lower sections and root systems of many of the trees scarred and infested by fungi. He could not predict how many years it would take for the trees to become dangerous, but he did claim "If a strong wind comes along there will be nothing left of Cathedral Grove."[136] Not wishing to detract from MacMillan's donation of the park, he added he was grateful the province had such a place as Cathedral Grove. Krajina had raised the concern because as a member of BCERC he had been working to have other areas of the province preserved, some with larger trees than Cathedral Grove.

Whenever logging encroached on the park, advocates publicly denounced the action. This was the case in the early seventies, when MB logging operations within the Cameron Valley came under attack. Adding fuel to concerns, MB Northwest Bay Division, south of Parksville, announced it would log 3000 acres near Cathedral Grove. The Port Alberni Chamber of Commerce proposed that a trade-off of land near Cathedral Grove be made for another logging area, to give the park a better windbreak. The area lay within Tree Farm 19, a 340,000-acre section of land owned by the company, and although privately owned, MB still had to conform to forestry service guidelines.

Despite declarations the company would leave a two-hundred-foot strip of trees near the highway along Cameron River and that no logging would come closer to the highway than 450 feet, the public was not reassured. Experienced loggers felt the proposed cutting would leave the park exposed to high winds. Letters were written to government and protests organized. The irony was that only a few years before, MB had proposed to the provincial government it extend the boundaries of MacMillan Park. The company proposed that "nearly 600 acres of its forest land extending from the top of the Hump to the park boundary and down to the Cameron River" should become part of the park.[137] There were estimates of about 130,000 mature trees in the whole area which included the proposed boundary extension.

There had been an agreement in principle that some form of compensation would be offered MB for the loss of this company-owned land and timber. The deal never was made to extend the park boundaries because, in the interim, there was a change in government in Victoria and discussions were stymied.

The Ministry of Forests approved the logging plans, and logging proceeded amidst public anguish at the perceived destruction clearly visible from the highway. Logging in the upper Cameron Valley removed the park's former buffer of trees. The blow-down threat to the park now became real. Today the area in question is slowly greening over with a new-growth forest.

Protests over logging in the area have diminished. Today the major concern is the growing number of visitors and limited parking. Highway 4 almost cuts the park in half, and in the summertime cars, campers, and trailers fight for any available parking alongside the roadway—a very dangerous situation indeed with the high volume of traffic heading west. The park is suffering from its growing popularity.

The short-term prognosis for the forest in the park is that the trees have many years of life left. There may be losses due to old age, root and stem rots, and windthrow due to strong down-valley winds. Also there could be further losses caused by water, and bank erosion from flash floods. The run-off following heavy winter rains is not intercepted by the former old-growth forest. This results in rapid runoff from the steep valley slopes and in downstream erosion.[138]

The long-term prognosis is for the Douglas-firs to be reduced and the remaining mixed forest to be dominated by western hemlock, western redcedar, and grand fir. But there will still be the occasional Douglas-fir regenerated in forest openings created by tree mortality and windthrow. The current age of the Douglas-fir varies from 450 to 800 years. This species has been recorded to live, on drier sites, to 1300 years. Global warming could also play a major role in the changes of the species in the forest.

A fallen tree becomes a step-bridge.

A lattice of branches.

Giant cedars thrive on the lake side of the park where normally moist conditions provide a perfect growing environment for the species.

The ground-cover of mixed seedlings and ferns.

The up-rooted
giants wind-blown.

A quiet walk through the grove.

Sadly this huge stump is all that remains of the 700-year-old redcedar.

A stand of first- and second-growth trees almost hides busy Highway 4.

Highway 4 winds through the park and usually is very busy.

Hoar frost on rocks near the river.

Many of these issues have been addressed in the B.C. Parks Master Plan, which will guide all future decisions made within the next few years. MacMillan Park-Cathedral Grove, continues to be one of the few remaining examples of Douglas-fir forests left in British Columbia and remains a source of joy to the residents of the Central Vancouver Island area who fought for so many years to have it preserved for future generations.

MacMillan's gift to the province is a living legacy to the people of British Columbia. And as he would have wished, the park provides an excellent opportunity to study the old-growth forest and to promote increased public knowledge and understanding of the forest.

DAVID DOUGLAS (1799-1834)

On July 22, 1984 a plaque was unveiled in the park to honour David Douglas, the Scottish botanist who gave his name to the Douglas-fir tree. The plaque rests among living monuments to nature, the magnificent firs of Cathedral Grove. Parks Canada and the provincial parks branch joined hundreds of people, including the mayors of Qualicum Beach, Parksville, and Port Alberni to dedicate this lasting memorial.[139]

Douglas, who died in an accident while exploring Hawaii in 1834, spent a significant portion of his short career investigating the flora of western North America. From his base at the Hudson's Bay Company post on the lower Columbia River he explored the western United States south to Spanish California, made two journeys into the interior of British Columbia, and once accompanied the fur trade brigade back to York Factory on Hudson Bay.

His accolades included several firsts: although suffering from arthritis, he became the first European to have climbed a Canadian Rocky mountain; the first to have scaled the Blue Mountains of Oregon, and the first to climb the Hawaiian peaks of Mauna Kea and Mauna Loa.

Douglas may have had many firsts but the tree that carries his name remains the constant reminder of the man. The Douglas-fir was among the 254 new species of plant life he discovered and identified during his short career. He named it *Pinus Taxifolia*. A test for durability proved the wood to be strong, tough, straight-grained, and durable. It became the world's greatest building wood.

DR. JAMES FLETCHER

Dr. James Fletcher became a highly respected colleague and Fellow of the Royal Society of Canada. When he died in 1908, the Canadian Forestry Association praised his work:

> The executive committee of the Canadian Forestry Association desires to place on record an expression of the sorrow which will be shared by all members of the Association at the death of Dr. James Fletcher. Dr. Fletcher took an active interest, before the formation of the Association, and on its organization became one of its active members and associated very materially in its work. The high place which Dr. Fletcher held in the scientific world and in the life of the Dominion of Canada cannot be easily filled. His scientific attainments, his helpfulness, his unfailing kindness and cheerfulness, made him known to a large circle of friends and it is with a feeling of personal loss that we wish to convey our sympathy to his sorrowing family and friends.[140]

Queen's University, in Kingston, Ontario, conferred an honourary degree upon him on April 29, 1896.[141] Fletcher was also one of the founders of the Ottawa Field Naturalists' Club. There is a monument erected in his honour at the Experimental Farm in Ottawa.

JAMES ROBERT ANDERSON

For thirty years, James Robert Anderson worked as a civil servant. He rose in rank to become the first Deputy Ministry of Agriculture, a position he held until ill health forced his retirement in 1908. A botanist, Anderson was also a keen student of natural history and one of the first members of the Natural History Society of British Columbia, founded in 1890. Birds, insects, rocks, and soil claimed most of his interests. But plant life, trees, shrubs, and flowers were his chief hobby. In 1925, the Department of Education published as a reference book for use in the schools of the province, Anderson's *Trees and Shrubs: Food, Medicinal, and Poisonous Plants of British Columbia*.[142]

Anderson donated many items of historic value to the provincial archives, including maps, photographs, old pamphlets and books, and a few curious relics such as the first set of chessmen used in British Columbia, which were carved by his father and contained in a pouch made from an eagle's claw.

On April 9, 1930, Anderson was struck by a car as he crossed the road and died immediately.

REVEREND GEORGE TAYLOR (1851-1912)

Reverend George Taylor, formerly a mining engineer from Derby, England, came to Canada in 1879 to visit a cousin and decided to stay.[143] He was ordained in the Anglican Church of British Columbia in 1884 and served parishes in Victoria, Ottawa, Ontario, and Wellington, B.C., a mining community north of Nanaimo.[144] From his home on Gabriola Island, in the area now known as Taylor Bay on the north side of the Island, he combed the beaches and coves, collecting specimens and noting information that would prove valuable to marine biologist and scientist alike. His work in this regard gained him entry as a Fellow of the prestigious Royal Society of Canada, the only member then living west of Winnipeg.

As a naturalist and entomologist, Taylor's study and concern for marine life led him to campaign for a Dominion Biological Station for British Columbia.[145] The station was established in Departure Bay, in Nanaimo in 1908. Taylor served as the first curator of the station until his death in August 1912.[146]

MARTIN ALLERDALE GRAINGER

Grainger, a graduate mathematician from Cambridge University and British Columbia's second chief forester, was a familiar figure in the high country between Hope and Princeton now known as Manning Park. He first discovered the area while on a horseback trip and was so captivated by its beauty he returned many times, even making trips on the Kettle Valley Railroad. When there was talk of opening up the area for development and building a highway from Hope to Princeton, Grainger and MacMillan played an active role in lobbying the government to preserve the area for a park. MacMillan thought the park would be named for his friend Grainger.

But as fate would have it, another chief forester at the time, E. C. Manning, was killed in a plane crash, and the government decided to name the park in his honour. Manning Park was officially dedicated with the completion of the highway in 1941. Within a few months, Grainger died of a heart attack at the age of sixty-six.

Grainger is remembered also for his writing of *Woodsmen of the West*, first published in 1908 and now reprinted, and for a collection of his writings preserved by his niece Evelyn and published in 1994 under the title *Riding the Skyline*.

ARTHUR WELLESLEY GRAY

Gray was born in New Westminster, B.C. on October 6, 1876. He married Margaret Heggie Arnot in 1914. They had two daughters. He entered municipal politics in 1907 serving first as alderman and then later as mayor of that city. In addition to his municipal duties, he found time to serve on many community, regional, and provincial boards. He was elected to the Provincial Legislature for New Westminster in a by-election in 1927, then re-elected in general elections in 1933 and 1937. In the Pattullo cabinet Wells Gray was appointed Minister of Lands.[147]

Perhaps the most lasting reminder of Wells Gray is the provincial park dedicated in his honour on November 28, 1939. The park, one of British Columbia's largest and most spectacular, is located 40 kilometres north of Clearwater and covers 527,307 hectares. It contains five major lakes, two large river systems, waterfalls, extinct volcanoes, and mineral springs.[148]

Notes

1 Sound Heritage. Vol. IV. Number 2. Aural History. Provincial Archives of British Columbia, 1975. "Four Poems from 'Emily,'" Florence McNeil.

2 G. P. V. Akrigg and Helen B. Akrigg, *British Columbia Place Names*, Sono Nis Press, 1986.

3 Master Plan for MacMillan Provincial Park, Ministry of Environment, Lands and Parks, 1992, p. 47.

4 *Ibid.*, p. 50.

5 *Ibid.*, p. 58.

6 David Kelly, Gary Braasch, *Secrets of the Old Growth Forest*, Gibbs Smith, Publisher, Layton, Utah, US, 1988, p. 9.

7 Ed Gould, *Logging, British Columbia's Logging History*, Hancock House, Publishers Ltd, 1975. p. 15.

8 Gilbert Malcolm Sproat journal 1868. *Scenes and Studies of Savage Life*, published in England by Smith, Elder and Co. p. 308.

9 *Ibid.* See also Adam Grant Horne file, Nanaimo Museum Archives.

10 Alfred Carmichael, *Indian Legends of Vancouver Island*, 1922. Ethnology Vol. 1, West Coast file. Alberni Valley Museum.

11 J. A. Costello file, *The Siwash: Their life legends and tales*. The Calvert Company, Seattle. Chapter 30, p. 115-21. Alberni Valley Museum.

12 Richard Mayne, *Four Years in British Columbia and Vancouver Island*, John Murray, Albemarie Street, London, England, 1862. p. 167-73.

13 W.Young, president, B. C. Forestry Association, paper *Forestry—A third Sector Response*, presented to a public meeting September 24, 1986 in Port Alberni. p. 6.

14 *Ibid.*

15 Jan Peterson, *The Albernis 1860-1922*, Oolichan Books, Lantzville, B.C. 1992, p. 27.

16 Craig Brown, *The Illustrated History of Canada*, Lester & Orpen Dennys Ltd., 1987, p. 239-41.

17 Kenneth & Alexandrina McKenzie file 25.4 ADHSA.

18 Maggie M. Paquet, *PARKS of British Columbia and the Yukon*, Maia Publishing Limited, North Vancouver, B.C., 1990, p. 1.

19 Ministry of Lands, Parks and Housing brochure, Trees of Cathedral Grove. 1980.

20 Report of Entomologist and Botanist James Fletcher, Sessional Paper No. 16, dated 1901, p. 207, ADHSA.

21 *Ibid.*, Chaper 3: Development of Divisions 1886-1913, Entomology and Botany Division.

22 J. R. Anderson Diary 1901. Add MSS 1912 V3 f.2. BCARS.

23 *Colonist*, October 12, 1930.

24 See Fletcher paper, p. 201.

25 *Ibid.*, p. 207.

26 Canadian Forestry Association minute book, Second Annual meeting March 7, 1901, p. 18. Also meeting of September 27, 1901, p. 22, drawing attention to the *Bush Fire Act* of British Columbia. National Archives of Canada.

27 Fletcher's letter to sister Flory, dated September 3, 1901. File 4.8.

28 Canadian Forestry Association, Constitution and bylaws drawn up and approved March 8, 1900.

29 *Ibid.*, March 5, 6, 1903, p. 40.

30 Ibid., March 10, 1904, p. 50.

31 Donald MacKay, *Empire of Wood, The MacMillan Bloedel Story*, Douglas & McIntyre, Vancouver. 1982. p. 26.

32 M. Allerdale Grainger, *Woodsmen of the West*, reprinted from 1908 edition in 1994 by Horsdal & Schubart Publishers Ltd., Victoria. p. 33.

33 *Alberni Pioneer News*, August 17, 1907.

34 *Nanaimo Daily Free Press*, July 21, 1973.

35 File L.15.7.3 #5, ADHSA.

36 File L.15.7.3 #10, ADHSA.

37 Ministry of Forests define old-growth forest as trees 30 metres or more in height and 150 years or more in age.

38 E. T. Buxton journal, director of the Red Cliff Land and Lumber Company Limited, 1907. Alberni Valley Museum.

39 *Ibid.*

40 *Alberni Pioneer News*, November 23, 1907.

41 *Ibid.*, June 3, 1911.

42 *Port Alberni News*, September 13, 1922 (Reprint of *Western Lumberman* article).

43 Undated newspaper clipping, "Diary of a Journey through Life." Henry Gerard Thornton was knighted in 1960 and died February 6, 1977.

44 *Nanaimo Daily Free Press*, July 21, 1973.

45 Ian Baird, *A Historic Guide to the E&N Railway*, 1985, published by Heritage Architectural Guides in association with the Friends of the E&N, Victoria, B.C. See also Robert D. Turner, *Vancouver Island Railroads*, 1973, Golden West Books, San Marino, California.

46 Western Canada Wilderness calendar date-sketchbook 1983.

47 Canadian Forestry Association minute book, February 11, 1909, p. 122.

48 *Ibid.*, September 4-6, 1912, p. 240-49.

49 MacKay, p. 21. The following information on H. R. MacMillan comes from this source.

50 *Ibid.*, p. 33.

51 See Grainger p. 210-11.

52 See Gould p. 63.

53 W. H. Olsen, *Water Over The Wheel*, Schutz Industries Ltd., Chemainus, 1981, p. 95-100.

54 Canadian Forestry Association minute book, February 4, 1914, p. 321.

55 *Ibid.*, January 19, 1915, p. 344.

56 *Ibid.*, January 20, 1916, p. 356.

57 *Ibid.*, January 15, 1917, p. 364.

58 See Grainger p. 213.

59 W. H. Olsen, *Water Over The Wheel*, Schutz Industries Ltd., 1981, p. 166.

60 *Ibid.*, p. 163.

61 *Ibid.*, p. 165.

62 *Vancouver Sun*, February 10, 1976.

63 *Port Alberni News*, December 24, 1919.

64 *Ibid.*

65 Port Alberni City Council minutes of Ordinary Council meeting, October 6, 1919. City of Port Alberni archives.

66 *Port Alberni News*, November 10, 1920.

67 *Ibid.*, February 9, 1921.

68 *Ibid.*, February 16, 1921.

69 *Ibid.*, February 9, 1921, p. 2.

70 *Ibid.*, April 6, 1921.

71 *Ibid.*, August 2, 1923.

72 *Nanaimo Daily Free Press*, July 21, 1973 p11. Article by John Cass.

73 See MacKay, p. 208.

74 See Olsen, p. 130.

75 *Port Alberni News*, October 24, 1923.

76 G. W. Taylor, *Timber: History of the Forest Industry in B.C.*, J. J. Douglas Ltd., Vancouver 1975. p. 70-72.

77 See MacKay, p. 94, 95.

78 *Ibid.*, p. 103.

79 Ralph S. Johnson, *Forests of Nova Scotia, a history*. Nova Scotia Department of Lands and Forests, 1986, p. 176-77.

80 File L.34.5. ADHSA. Information from the Directory of MLA's of Nova Scotia, p. 23, prepared by the Public Archives of Nova Scotia, 1958. See also letter from daughter Mrs. Leonora B. Wood, Kingfield, Maine, dated February 21, 1958. See also Johnson.

81 File ML 100, Vol. 108, p. 12, Public Archives of Nova Scotia. On the occasion of his death the following information was reported in the *Halifax Chronicle*, February 21, 1933.

82 See Johnson, p. 176.

83 *Port Alberni News*, August 23, 1928.

84 Qualicum Beach Board of Trade minute book, August 8, 1928; courtesy Qualicum Beach Chamber of Commerce.

85 *Port Alberni News*, August 23, 1928.

86 B.C. Parks archives. Letter dated July 28, 1929.

87 *Ibid*. Memorandum dated July 17, 1984. File 6-2-010.

88 B. A. Botkin, *A Treasury of Southern Folklore*, Crown Publishers, New York. p. 149-52

89 Bernard Devoto, *A Treasury of Western Folklore*, Crown Publishers, Inc., New York. p. 69.

90 Janez Stanonik, *Moby Dick: The Myth and the Symbol*, Ljubljana University Press, 1962. p. 108.

91 See Akrigg.

92 *West Coast Advocate*, February 6, 1936.

93 *Ibid.*, February 13, 1936.

94 Canadian Pacific Archives, File No. RG4 #16517. Letter dated July 25, 1936.

95 *Ibid*. Lord Tweedsmuir's letter to Elizabeth Constance MacKenzie, Local Council of Women, dated September 24, 1936, on the occasion of the visit of His Excellency, August 1936.

96 *West Coast Advocate*, March 5, 1936.

97 *Ibid.*, March 12, 1936 (Pacific News Services).

98 B.C. Parks archives.

99 *West Coast Advocate*, July 2, 1936.

100 *Port Alberni News*, May 22, 1930.

101 *Ibid.*, November 6, 1930.

102 Canadian Pacific Archives, File No. RG4 #16517. Letter dated April 14, 1937.

103 *Ibid.*, April 15, 1937.

104 *Ibid.*, September 22, 1937.

105 Patricia Marchak, *Green Gold, The Forest Industry in British Columbia*, University of British Columbia Press, Vancouver, 1983, p. 94.

106 *West Coast Advocate*, November 30, 1939.

107 See MacKay, p. 138.

108 See Taylor, p. 158.

109 *West Coast Advocate*, November 9, 1939.

110 See MacKay, p. 142.

111 *Alberni District News*, June 6, 1940.

112 See Taylor, p. 157.

113 *West Coast Advocate*, April 3, 1941.

[114] See Paquet, p. 34, 36.

[115] *West Coast Advocate*, March 13, 1941.

[116] *Ibid.*, July 9, 1942.

[117] *Ibid.*, July 16, 1942.

[118] *Ibid.*, August 6, 1942.

[119] Canadian Pacific Archives, File No. RG4 #16517.

[120] *Ibid.*, October 21, 1943.

[121] B.C. Parks archives.

[122] See MacKay p. 151.

[123] *Ibid.*, p. 152.

[124] See CP Archives. April 27, 1944.

[125] *Ibid.*, September 28, 1944.

[126] University of British Columbia, The Library, Special Collections Division, MacMillan Bloedel Ltd Records, Dorothy Dee Scrapbooks re H. R. MacMillan, Box 467, file #8.

[127] *Ibid.* Other letters of praise come from this source.

[128] See MacKay p. 113-14.

[129] See UBC collections, Box 467, file #8.

[130] *Ibid.* H. R. MacMillan Export Company inter-company correspondence dated June 12, 1946.

[131] See MacKay p. 156.

[132] See Taylor, p. 169-70.

[133] *West Coast Advocate*, August 7, 1947.

[134] See *Parks*, p. 1.

[135] *Vancouver Sun*, August 5, 1972.

[136] *Alberni Valley Times*, December 31, 1973.

[137] *Ibid.*, March 26, 1974.

[138] The short- and long-term prognosis on the park is from Kerry Joy, B.C. Parks Forester.

[139] *Alberni Valley Times*, July 17, 23, 1984.

[140] Canadian Forestry Association (CFA) minute book, November 20, 1908, p. 100. National Archives of Canada.

[141] Queen's University Archives, Kingston, Ontario.

[142] Civil Service Newsletter, March 1966. Pioneer Builders of British Columbia. BCARS.

[143] June Lewis-Harrison, *The People of Gabriola*, 1982, p. 95.

[144] *Nanaimo Free Press*, August 23, 1912. Nanaimo Archives.

[145] *The Gabriola Sounder*, November 30, 1993. Nanaimo Archives.

[146] See Lewis-Harrison, p. 102.

[147] S. M. Carter, *Who's Who in British Columbia*, 1939, p. 45.

[148] See Paquet, p. 60.

PART II

A stand of Douglas-fir.

TREES OF
CATHEDRAL GROVE

*T*he forests play a vital role in the lives of British Columbians. From the beginning of the province's history, Native people used the trees for canoes, houses, fuel, tools, beds, clothing and medicines. Today, trees are still considered a valuable resource; in different forms they are transported by truck, rail, and ship to every corner of the world.

MacMillan Park (Cathedral Grove) is considered an "old-growth" forest, a definition still under considerable debate amongst foresters and scientists. Ministry of Forests inventory maps define old-growth forests as trees 30 metres or more in height and 150 years or more in age. The park is one of the last remaining areas of old-growth forest on a major British Columbia highway. As a consequence, it is the most accessible and most visited by the public. In the seventies, a report released by the Ministry of Forests noted the heavily used trails showed signs of widening and wear to the point where tree roots had become exposed and were subject to wounding. The 1992 B.C. Parks Master Plan has identified ways of improving this situation.

There are fifteen different tree species located within the park. The rate at which trees grow is dependent on age, the competition for space, and the climate and soil conditions required by the species. The main constituents in the park are the four coniferous trees, the Douglas-fir, western hemlock, western redcedar, and to a lesser extent the grand fir, and two deciduous trees, the broadleaf maple and the red alder. Of course, there are other trees in the park; these include the black cottonwood, western yew, arbutus, western flowering dogwood, Sitka willow, paper birch, and western white pine.

Douglas-fir

Pseudotsuga menziesii

Within Cathedral Grove, the largest trees are the magnificent eight-hundred-year-old Douglas-firs, which survived a forest fire that swept through the area three hundred years ago. Most of the other trees are "youngsters" that have grown up since the fire. The greatest tree in the park measures three metres in diameter, or just a shade over nine metres in circumference. It would take six adults holding hands to encircle this monarch. The height of this tree is 75 metres. Except for the redwoods, the Douglas-fir is the tallest of all North American trees. The tallest tree in Canada is a 95-metre Sitka spruce in Carmanah Park.

Douglas-firs are evergreens with single needles arranged spirally around the branchlets. Mature trees have thick, greyish bark broken vertically into irregular broad ridges separated by deep "V"-shaped crevices. The bark, often over 30 centimetres thick, helps to protect the tree from fire. The root system is strong and wide-spreading, which makes the tree very windfirm. Some trees will survive for more than a thousand years. Douglas-firs are pioneer species, intolerant of shade. They will eventually be replaced in the park by western hemlock, western redcedar, and grand fir.

The reproductive parts consist of both male and female organs in separate cones on the same tree. The female cones are most commonly seen. They are, when mature, from 10 to 20 centimetres long and are easily distinguished from other cones by the prominent three-pronged bracts which extend beyond the edges of the scales.

Scientists have estimated there are three hundred species of insects associated with a fallen, decomposing Douglas-fir. These range from wood-chewing insects such as beetles, ants, and termites to debris eaters like earthworms, mites, and earwigs.

The wood of the Douglas-fir was once used by Native peoples to make spear handles, harpoon shafts, salmon weirs, and cod hooks. The pitch was used as a sealing and caulking agent for canoes, and was also used as a medicinal salve for wounds and skin irritations.

Western redcedar *Thuja plicata*

is British Columbia's provincial tree. It is easily recognized by the scaly leaves pressed to the twigs, and the thin, stringy bark. Its branches tend to spread or droop slightly and then turn upward. The bark is grey to reddish brown.

The reddish fragrant wood has been named "the cornerstone of north-west coast Indian culture"; the wood could be easily split and was rot-

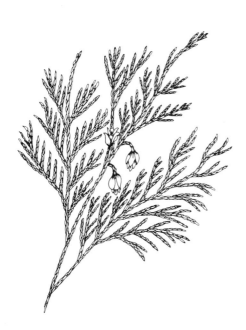

resistant, making it an ideal medium in making dugout canoes, house planks, posts and totem poles. It was also an excellent fuel for drying fish because it burns with little smoke. The bark was highly prized for making baskets, clothing and mats.

The cedar is also said to have some mythical quali-ties, its power so strong that a person could receive strength just by standing with his or her back to the tree. Also called the "tree of life," the tree is held in high esteem by all northwest coast tribes for its healing and spiritual powers. A Coast Salish myth says the Great Spirit created redcedar in honour of a man who was always helping others; "When he dies and where he is buried, a cedar tree will grow and be useful to the people—the roots for baskets, the bark for clothing, the wood for shelter." (Hilary Stewart, *Cedar: Tree of Life*, p. 27)

Western hemlock *Tsuga heterophylla*

grow abundantly on the shaded forest floor and can be easily recognized by their lacy foliage and droopy tops. The bark is rough, reddish-brown, and scaly. The needles are short, flat, blunt, and widely spaced at unequal lengths of five to twenty centimetres long, producing feathery flat sprays.

These young trees often start growing on the tops of stumps and fallen logs. The bark was once used as a tanning agent for colouring wool or

115

baskets. The Nuu-chah-nulth used the hemlock branches for collecting herring spawn. Hemlock branches were considered an excellent bedding material, as well. The tree has medicinal qualities valued by Coast Indians. Hemlock pitch was applied for a variety of purposes, including poultices, linaments, or, when mixed with deer tallow, as a salve to prevent sunburn. Hemlock bark tea, mixed with the bark of cascara and red alder, was considered beneficial for internal injuries.

Grand fir or balsam *Abies grandis*

is found throughout the Grove. One grand fir is more than 3.5 metres around, and has a height of nearly 61 metres. It is easily distinguished from other true firs by its sprays of lustrous needles in two distinct rows. The flat needles are usually spread so horizontally that both the upper and lower sides of the branches are clearly visible. The grand fir can usually be found beneath the Douglas-fir and is very sensitive to fire. The

bark is greyish-brown, usually with white mottles, smooth with resin blisters when young, becoming ridged and then scaly with age.

A brown dye made from the bark was used in basketry. Balsam knots were shaped, steamed, and carved into halibut hooks and other types of fish hooks by coastal tribes. The bark, when mixed with stinging nettles, was considered a general tonic, and its needles made a medicinal tea for colds.

The name "grand" was given to the tree by botanist David Douglas because it was straight and grew 80 metres tall. It is sometimes called the "stinking fir" because its crushed leaves give off a strong balsamy, or "catty" odour.

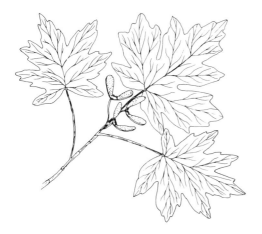

Broadleafed maple

Acer macrophyllum

is one of the few deciduous trees in the Grove. Its large leaves, 20 to 30 centimetres long, are divided into five prominent lobes. This tree often reaches heights of over 30 metres. Often the bark is not visible because of the mosses and other plant life that thrive on it. Sometimes the mosses get so thick they can form a "soil" into which trees root, sprout, and grow.

The broadleafed maple was called the "paddle tree" because the wood was used to make paddles. The giant leaves were good for making temporary containers. Even the sap could be used as a type of maple syrup. Preparations from the tree could treat sore throats.

How a tree grows

Trees grow in all directions at once. The crown, which is the tree's growth generator, is powered by the sun's energy. Every year it adds a new leader and a whorl of branches at the top of the stem. Lower branches increase in length, creating a shell of new foliage. Below ground, the root tips, protected against abrasion by a tough outer layer, reach outward and downward, growing thicker and longer in proportion to above-ground growth. Tiny root hairs absorb moisture and nutrients. Tree growth actually originates in the cambium, which is a layer of living cells separating the wood and bark.

The inner side of the cambium produces new layers of sapwood, or zylem; the outer side of the cambium produces inner bark, or phloem. The sapwood conducts water and nutrients from the roots to the tree leaves or needles. Here, the process of photosynthesis produces the tree's life-sustaining sugars. These sugars are returned through the inner bark to the tree's growth areas in the stem, branches, and roots. The inner bark dies and becomes outer bark—protection against pests, heat, cold, and injury. Old sapwood becomes dead heartwood. The sapwood cells that

117

are added each spring are big and pale; late summer's cells are smaller and darker. The colour difference reveals the growth ring for that year.

The silent power of the trunk

A raindrop falls to the forest floor, trickles through the debris, and soon is absorbed by the fir tree's root system. Two hours later a particle from that droplet has worked its way through the tree trunk to a needle at the end of a branch nearly twenty storeys above the ground. The trunk of a tree channels water and nutrients to the tree's needles (or leaves). In order for photosynthesis to take place, the tree trunk must support and position the leaves to gain maximum benefit from available light; it must transport water and minerals from the roots upward to the leaves, and it must carry the manufactured sugar and proteins back to areas of growth and repair.

A complete explanation for the upward movement of water through the trunk has eluded scientists for years. The most commonly accepted theory is based on the tendency of water molecules to stick together, a phenomenon readily apparent to anyone watching water bead up on a freshly waxed car. As a leaf loses water to the air through evaporation (transpiration), other water molecules within the leaf shift to fill the vacated spaces. In so doing they drag along more water molecules behind them, creating an unbroken string of water molecules extending all the way up from the roots.

Botanists estimate that a pressure of twenty to twenty-five atmospheres is required to pull sap to the top of British Columbia's tallest trees. This is about the pressure you would need to drink rootbeer through a straw almost three football fields long. The lifting power of the tree is even more impressive when you consider that 1000 kilograms of water are required to produce one kilogram of tree. For a Douglas-fir to grow to be two metres in diameter and 65 metres tall, its vascular system must effect a transportation of water roughly equivalent to raising a B.C. ferry to the top of the Empire State Building.

Tree trunks are the superstructure of the forest; sculptured pillars, rough, solid and graceful. Their silent beauty gives little hint of the dynamic forces at work within.

Information about the trees in Cathedral Grove has been gathered from several sources: the brochure: *Trees of Cathedral Grove*, published by Ministry of Lands, Parks and Housing, 1980; from Jim Pojar and Andy MacKinnon's *Plants of Coastal British Columbia*, published by the B.C. Ministry of Forests and Lone Pine Publishing, 1994; from Hilary Stewart's *Cedar: Tree of Life*, Douglas & McIntyre, 1984; and *Forest Talk Resource Magazine*, Summer 1982. Ministry of Forests, Victoria, B.C. p. 10, 22.

PLANTS OF
CATHEDRAL GROVE

*T*he B.C. Parks 1982 Ecosystems study of MacMillan Park provides a detailed list of 16 shrubs and 118 herbs, along with their scientific names and common names. The list is a regular cornucopia of wonderful names like black swamp gooseberry, Pacific trailing blackberry, common snowberry, wild ginger, licorice fern, cow parsnip, wood strawberry, willow herb, wall-lettuce, and field mint, to name only a few.

Identified in ten distinct plant associations are sword fern, vanilla leaf, foamflower, maidenhair fern, enchanter's nightshade, lady fern (2), skunk cabbage, meadow horsetail, and Pacific Oenanthe. At present there is no evidence Cathedral Grove was ever used by Native people, but the plants, shrubs, and herbs growing within are common to other areas of Vancouver Island and the Coast. Information about their use has been provided for general interest and enjoyment of the park.

Sword fern

Polystichum munitum

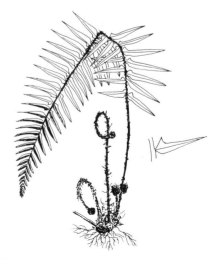

grows about 1.5 metres tall and covers approximately 20 per cent of the park mainly along the northwest side on the slope of Mt. Horne. The stem is straw-coloured with flaking scales, and its leaflets are leathery, long and narrow, sharp-pointed, serrated, large toothed at base, and attached to the stem by a small short stalk.

Native people found good uses

for the sword fern. In the spring, the large rhizomes (subterranean stems) were eaten as a starvation food by several tribes. They were roasted over a fire or steamed in a traditional pit oven, then peeled and eaten. The Nuu-chah-nulth ate the cooked rhizomes especially when needed to cure diarrhea. Sword fern was also known as the "pala-pala" plant, because children played a game to see who could pull the most leaflets off a leaf in a single breath while saying "pala" with each one.

Vanilla leaf

Achlys triphylla

occupies approximately 40 per cent of the park and covers most of the valley floor. The plant prefers dry to moist conditions and nutrient-medium to very rich soil. The single erect stem is characterized by a single large leaf divided into three leaflets that are almost triangular in shape with outer edge rounded and wavy. The separate flowering stem from the base has a cluster of numerous small white flowers at the top of the stem. *Achlys* means "mist" and is thought to describe the misty clouds of tiny white flowers.

Vanilla leaf leaves have been used as insect repellents. The leaves were often dried and hung in bunches to perfume the house with their sweet vanilla scent.

Foamflower

Tiarella trifoliata

can be found in the north central area adjacent to the south of the central parking lot. It can also be found in isolated patches along the river bank. Covering about 10 per cent of the park area, the plant prefers moist, shady coniferous forests, or streambanks. The perennial plant has glandular-hairy erect stems that

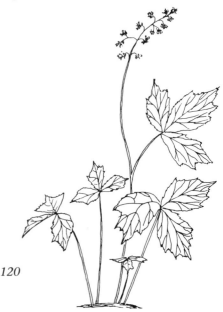

120

grow about 15-60 centimetres tall with slender, short rhizomes. The leaves have long stalks with three leaflets that are irregularly lobed and coarsely toothed. The flowers are tiny, delicate white clusters at the end of short wire-like stalks. The name is Latin for "tiara," which was a turban-like head-dress of ancient Persians, not the glittering diamond headdress worn by royalty.

The *Tiarella* species are named "foamflowers" because the flowers appear like specks of foam, sometimes called "sugar-scoops" in reference to the unusual shape of the opened capsules.

Maidenhair fern

Aadiantum pedatum

grows to heights of 60 centimetres and has a fan-shaped appearance. Stems range in colour from black to reddish-brown and shiny, forking at the top with each branch arching upward then curing downward. This fern prefers a moist to wet environment, on rocky forests, streambanks, and low elevations.

Like many of the other plants, the Indians found medicinal qualities in the leaves for strength and endurance. European herbalists also used the maidenhair fern to make cough medicine.

Enchanter's nightshade

Circaea alpina

is of the evening primrose family. The leaves are short-stalked, with pointed tips, and shaped like a heart or an egg. The small flowers are white to pale pink, and grow in clusters of eight to twelve on top of a long stalk.

Circaea is named after the Greek goddess Circe—an enchantress—who supposedly used the plant in powder form to lure prospective admirers.

Lady fern   *Athyrium filix-femina*

grows mainly along the floodplain of the Cameron River across the north portion of the park to the low terrace in the south central area, preferring moist to wet soil. The fern stands erect and spreads to about two metres tall. The stems are straw coloured; the branches are widest at mid-stem, the leaflets lobed and serrated, with twenty to forty pairs, tapering towards the base and tip, giving a diamond-shaped outline.

The fiddleheads of the fern were eaten in the early spring when they were 5-15 centimetres tall. They were boiled, baked, or eaten raw with grease.

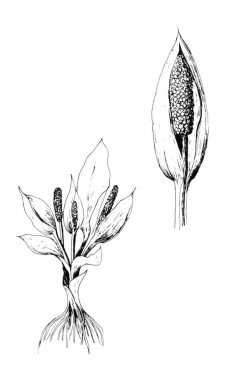

Skunk cabbage

Lysichiton americanum

is sometimes called the swamp lantern. Found along the Cameron River mouth, the plant likes wet, rich soil. It is most easily recognized by its large thick oval-shaped leaves. The stem is short, thick and erect, and gives off a smelly odour, especially when flowering. The flowers are yellowish-green in colour, small, and contained in a dense cluster on the flesh stalk surrounded by a yellow hood-like sheath.

The large oval leaves of the plant were used as Indian wax paper for lining berry baskets, berry-drying racks, and steaming pits. Skunk cabbage was used by the northwest coast Indians as a food in the early spring when food was scarce, and then only after steaming or roasting. Bears like to dig these plants up.

Meadow horsetail

Equisetum pratense

prefers forests, swamps, bog edges, and clearings, from low lands to alpine areas. *Equisetum* is from the Latin *"equus,"* meaning horse, and "setum" meaning bristle. Horsetails are an ancient group of plants that grew to the size of trees when dinosaurs roamed the earth.

There are other horsetail herbs in the park: the swamp, common, and giant varieties. The horsetails are rhizomatous herbs

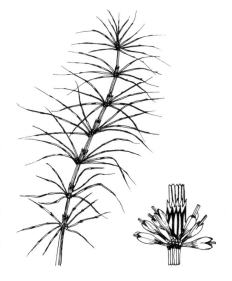

with aerial, usually hollow, grooved, regularly jointed stems impregnated with silica, which makes them harsh to the touch.

Ancient Romans ate young, fertile common-horsetail shoots as if they were asparagus. They also used them as tea and as a thickening powder. Common horsetail is one of the most widespread plants in the world, and it often turns up as a bad garden weed, sometimes called "devil guts." It was the first vascular plant to send green shoots up through the debris of the 1980 eruption of Mt. St. Helens.

Devil's Club

Oplopanax horridus

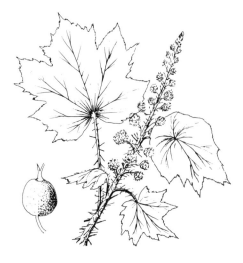

prefers moist to wet conditions. It has large serrated maple-leaf shaped leaves, with spines on the underside veins. It grows to 3 metres tall and has a thick, yellowish, heavily spined stem.

The shrub is related to ginseng, and is still regarded as the most important of all medicinal plants. Arthritis, ulcers, digestive tract ailments, and diabetes were treated with devil's club. Tea made from the inner bark is taken by many people today for diabetes. Devil's club sticks are used by Native people as protective charms, and charcoal from burned devil's club is used to make a protective face paint for dancers and others who are ritually vulnerable to evil influences. The lightweight wood was used for making fishing lures.

Salmonberry   *Rubus spectabilis*

is a common, moderately shade-tolerant deciduous shrub that grows 4 metres tall from branching rhizomes, often forming dense thickets. The bark is golden-brown and the raspberry-shaped fruit is often a peachy orange, yellow, or red colour. The shrub likes moist to wet conditions, along the river edge, in the forest, or in wet logged areas. Both the sprouts and the berries can be eaten. The young stem sprouts are gathered in the spring as a green vegetable. They are peeled or eaten raw, and sometimes steamed. Opinions vary as to the tastiness of the berries, which often give the appearance of mushy raspberries.

Salmonberries are the earliest berries to ripen. Patches of these berries were often owned by families or individuals. A Nuu-chah-nulth salmon-berry patch was harvested exclusively by the owner until enough boxes were collected to hold a feast, after which the patch was harvested by all. Young shoots of the salmonberry bush  which come out in May are, when eaten with decayed salmon-roe, considered a most delicious dish.

Salal

Gaultheria shallon

is the most common forest shrub in the region and grows in most coniferous forest thickets, rocky cliffs, ravines, and exposed shores. The shrub spreads by lay-ering, suckering, and sprouting; its height varies from 0.2 to 5 metres tall. Leaves are thick and leathery. Flowers grow in clusters and are whitish-pink. The fruit is black, hairy, and berry-like in appearance.

With the exception of seafood, there is no food so important to the Coast Natives as the salal berry. During the month of August it is gathered in great quantities; the berries are made into a syrup or dried in cakes, or they can be eaten fresh. They also can be made into jam.

Salal was a favourite of David Douglas, who brought seed to Britain in 1828 for use as a garden ornamental.

125

Oregon Grape

Mahonia nervosa

likes dry to fairly moist, open to closed forests at low to middle elevations. This evergreen stiff-branched shrub grows to 60 centimetres tall, with leaves like holly. No other shrub in the province bears any resemblance to it. Flowers are bright yellow and fruit berries blue in colour. The tart berries were often mixed with salal or some other sweeter fruit. Today they are used for jelly, and some people make wine from them. The bark and berries were also used medicinally for liver, gall-bladder, and eye problems.

Information about the plants has been gathered from several sources, namely the following: the study *Ecosystems of MacMillan Park on Vancouver Island*, Land Management report number 12, by A. E. Inselberg, K. Klinka and C. Ray, published by the Ministry of Forests, March 1982; *Master Plan for MacMillan Provincial Park*, published by Ministry of Environment, Lands and Parks, June 1992; Jim Pojar and Andy MacKinnon, *Plants of Coastal British Columbia*, published by the B.C. Ministry of Forests and Lone Pine Publishing, 1994, plus various other brochures and leaflets published by Ministry of Forests; T. M. C. Taylor, *The Ferns and Fern-allies of British Columbia*, University of British Columbia, 1956; A. E. Szcawinski and G. A. Hardy, *Guide to Common Edible Plants of British Columbia*, British Columbia Provincial Museum, 1962; and C. P. Lyons, *Trees, Shrubs and Flowers to know in British Columbia*, J. M. Dent & Sons (Canada) Limited, Vancouver, 1952.

Pen and ink illustrations of trees and plants are by Jan Peterson.

Bibliography

The author wishes to acknowledge assistance received from the following:

Alberni District Historical Society Archives

Alberni Valley Museum;

British Columbia Archives and Records Service

Canadian Forestry Association

Canadian Pacific Limited

MacMillan Bloedel Limited

MacMillan Bloedel Ltd., Alberni Forestry Information Centre, Port Alberni

Ministry of Environment Lands and Parks

Nanaimo Museum archives

National Archives of Canada

Port Alberni City archives

Public Archives of Nova Scotia

Qualicum Beach Board of Trade

Queen's University Archives, Kingston, Ontario

Vancouver Island Regional Library, Port Alberni

Victoria Natural History Society

University of British Columbia, Special Collections Division

Books

Akrigg, G. P. V. and Helen B. *British Columbia Coast Names*, Sono Nis Press, 1986.

Baird, Ian. *A Historic Guide to the E&N Railway*, Heritage Architectural Guides in association with Friends of the E&N. Victoria, B.C. 1985.

Botkin, B. A. *A Treasury of Southern Folklore*, Crown Publishers, New York.

Brown, Craig. *The Illustrated History of Canada*, Lester & Orpen Dennys Limited, Toronto, Ontario, 1987.

Carmichael, Alfred. *Indian Legends of Vancouver Island*, 1922.

Costello, J. A. *The Siwash: Their life, legends and tales*, The Calvert Company, Seattle.

Devoto, Bernard. *A Treasury of Western Folklore*, Crown Publishers, Inc., New York.

Gould, Ed. *Logging, British Columbia's Logging History*, Hancock House Publishers Ltd., 1975.

Grainger, M. Allerdale. *Woodsmen of the West*, Horsdal & Schubart Publishers Limited, Victoria, 1994. (Reprinted from 1908 edition.)

Johnson, Ralph S. *Forests of Nova Scotia, a history*, Nova Scotia Department of Lands and Forests, 1986.

Kelly, David and Gary Braasch. *Secrets of the Old Growth Forest*, Salt Lake City, Utah: Peregrine Smith Books, 1988.

Lewis-Harrison, June. *The People of Gabriola*, printed by D. W. Friesen & Sons Ltd., Cloverdale, B.C. 1982.

Marchak, Patricia. *Green Gold, The Forest Industry in British Columbia*, University of British Columbia Press, Vancouver, 1983.

Mayne, Richard. *Four Years in British Columbia and Vancouver Island*, John Murray, Albemarie Street, London, England, 1862.

MacKay, Donald. *Empire of Wood, The MacMillan Bloedel Story*, Douglas & McIntyre, Vancouver, 1982.

Ministry of Environment, Lands and Parks. *MacMillan Provincial Park Master Plan*, 1992.

Ministry of Forests. *Ecosystems of MacMillan Park on Vancouver Island*, 1982.

Nova Scotia Public Archives. *Directory of MLAs of Nova Scotia*, 1958

Olsen, W. H. *Water Over the Wheel*, Schutz Industries Ltd., Chemainus, 1981.

Paquet, Maggie M. *Parks of British Columbia & The Yukon*, Maia Publishing Limited, North Vancouver, B.C., 1990.

Peterson, Jan. *The Albernis 1860-1922*, Oolichan Books, Lantzville, B.C., 1992.

———. *Twin Cities, Alberni-Port Alberni*, Oolichan Books, Lantzville, B.C., 1994.

Pojar, Jim and MacKinnon, Andy. *Plants of Coastal British Columbia*, Lone Pine Publishing, Vancouver, 1994.

Sound Heritage, Volume IV, Number 2. *Four Poems from "Emily,"* Florence McNeil, 1975.

Sproat, Gilbert Malcolm. *Scenes and Studies of Savage Life*, Smith, Elder and Co., England, 1868.

Stanonik, Janez. *Moby Dick: The Myth and the Symbol*, Ljubljana University Press, 1962.

Stewart, Hilary. *Cedar: Tree of Life*, Douglas & McIntyre, 1984.

Taylor, G. W. *Timber: History of the Forest Industry in B.C.*, J. J. Douglas Limited, Vancouver, 1975.

Turner, Robert D. *Vancouver Island Railroads*, Golden West Books, San Marino, California, 1973.

Newspapers and Magazines

Alberni District News

Alberni Pioneer News

Alberni Valley Times

Colonist

Forest Talk Resource Magazine

Halifax Chronicle

Nanaimo Daily Free Press

Port Alberni News

Vancouver Sun

West Coast Advocate

Western Lumberman

Diaries, Journals, Letters

Anderson, J. R. Diary, 1901. Add MSS 1912 V3 f.2.BCARS.

Buxton, E. T. Journal, Director of Red Cliff Land and Lumber Company Limited, 1907.

Fletcher, James. Letter to sister Flory, 1901.

Lord Tweedsmuir. Letter to Elizabeth Constance MacKenzie, Local Council of Women, 1936. Canadian Pacific Archives, File No. RG4 #16517.

Thornton, Henry Gerard. "Diary of a Journey through Life."

Wood, Mrs. Leonora B. Letter re Frank J. D. Barnjum, 1958.

Minute books, papers, brochures

Canadian Forestry Association minute books.

Fletcher, James. Report of Entomologist and Botanist, *Sessional Paper No. 16*, 1901.

Ministry of Lands, Parks and Housing. Brochure, *Trees of Cathedral Grove*, 1980.

Port Alberni City Council minute book.

Qualicum Beach Board of Trade minute book.

Young, W. Paper, President of British Columbia Forestry Association, *Forestry-A Third Sector Response*, public meeting at Port Alberni, September 24, 1986.

Index

Jan Peterson spent her early life on a farm in Scotland, emigrating to Kingston, Ontario in 1957. With her husband Ray Peterson and three children she moved to the Alberni Valley in 1972. She has worked as a reporter for *The Alberni Valley Times* and published the Community Arts Council newsletter. She is the author of two books on the history of the Alberni Valley: *The Albernis* and *Twin Cities*. Both were published by Oolichan Books.